EDUCATION IN EUROPE

III–3 *Training the Trainer* (2nd edition revised and supplemented, 1966).

III–4 *Leisure-time Facilities for Young People from* 13 *to* 25 *Years of Age* (1965).

III–5 *Workers in Adult Education: Their Status, Recruitment, and Professional Training* (1966).

Section IV GENERAL (SUBJECTS OTHER THAN THOSE INCLUDED IN SECTIONS I, II, and III,—e.g., MODERN LANGUAGE TEACHING, FILM AND TELEVISION, etc.)

IV–1 *Recent Developments in Modern Language Teaching* (1964).

IV–2 *New Trends in Linguistic Research* (1963).

IV–3 *Research and Techniques for the Benefit of Modern Language Teaching* (1964).

IV–4 *Modern Language Teaching by Television* (1965).

IV–5 *Educational and Cultural Films: Experiments in European Co-Production* (1965).

IV–6 *Europe's Guests: Students and Trainees* (1966).

IV–7 *Art of the Cinema in Ten European Countries* (1967).

IV–8 *The Use of Short* 8-*mm. Films in European Schools* (1967).

IV–9 *Direct Teaching by Television* (1967).

Numbers I-6 to I-9 and II-11 and II-13 are published by George G. Harrap & Co. Ltd. Earlier numbers were published by the Council of Europe and are on sale at its sales agents listed at the end of this book.

Each volume is published in English and in French. The French edition of the present work is entitled *Les différents pays d'Europe vus par leurs géographes.*

COUNCIL FOR CULTURAL
CO-OPERATION OF THE
COUNCIL OF EUROPE

EDUCATION IN EUROPE
Section II – General and Technical Education

The Countries of Europe
as seen by their Geographers

compiled by
E. C. MARCHANT

GEORGE G. HARRAP & CO. LTD
London · Toronto · Wellington · Sydney

First published in Great Britain 1970
by GEORGE G. HARRAP & CO. LTD
182-184 High Holborn, London, W.C.1

© *Council of Europe* 1970

ISBN 0 245 50322 6

*Composed in Times type and printed at
the Pitman Press, Bath
Made in Great Britain*

Foreword

The series of publications *Education in Europe* was launched by the Council for Cultural Co-operation of the Council of Europe in 1963 in order to make known the comparative studies and surveys produced under its twenty-one nation programme of educational co-operation.

The Council of Europe was established by ten nations on May 5th, 1949, since when its membership has progressively increased to eighteen. Its aim is "to achieve a greater unity between its members for the purpose of safeguarding and realizing the ideals and principles which are their common heritage and facilitating their economic and social progress". This aim is pursued by discussion of questions of common concern and by agreements and common action in economic, social, cultural, scientific, legal, and administrative matters.

The Council for Cultural Co-operation was set up by the Committee of Ministers of the Council of Europe on January 1st, 1962, to draw up proposals for the cultural policy of the Council of Europe, to co-ordinate and give effect to the over-all cultural programme of the organization, and to allocate the resources of the Cultural Fund. It is assisted by three permanent committees of senior officials: for higher education and research (this committee also includes representatives of universities), for general and technical education, and for out-of-school education. All the member Governments of the Council of Europe, together with Finland, Spain, and the Holy See, which have acceded to the European Cultural Convention, are represented on these bodies.

Between 1963 and 1967 some 25 titles were published in English and French versions under the responsibility of the Council of Europe. Lists of these titles and of the Council's sales agents are given at the beginning and end of this book. In addition a number of reports of a more technical nature on educational and cultural problems have been produced in a separate series from 1965 onwards.

The Council of Europe ceded the world rights relating to the series *Education in Europe* as from January 1st, 1968, to George G. Harrap & Co. Ltd, London, for the English edition and to Armand Colin, Paris, for the French edition. These publishers are responsible throughout the world for the production, sale, and distribution of studies published by them in the series, which is divided into four sections:

I. Higher Education and Research (education at university level).
II. General and Technical Education (primary and secondary—including technical, commercial, and vocational—education).
III. Out-of-school Education and Youth (youth activities; adult education; physical education, sport, and outdoor pursuits).
IV. General (subjects other than those included in the three sections mentioned above).

The more technical reports will continue to be published in Strasbourg.

The opinions expressed in all these studies are not to be regarded as reflecting the policy of individual Governments or of the Committee of Ministers of the Council of Europe.

Preface

Between 1961 and 1964 the Council of Europe organized four conferences on the revision of geography textbooks and atlases; the final report on these conferences appeared in 1967 published in the collection *Education in Europe*, Section II–9[1], following an earlier publication *History Teaching and History Textbook Revision*, Section II–8.

When faced during these conferences with the task of passing judgment on the presentation of their country in foreign texts, "some reviewers, with good reason, decided that the only means of establishing their general criticism was to give an up-to-date account of the geography of their country as they thought it should be portrayed." Such accounts were rather long for the published summary report, but they were so clearly valuable that the reviewers were asked to confine their comments for the report to matter of criticism, and to put together, for separate publication, a positive account of their own country as they would like to see it represented in the textbooks of other countries. This volume of essays is the result of that suggestion.

Following another recommendation of the conferences, a volume of *Europe in Pictures* is to be published by Macmillan in co-operation with publishers in other countries. Photographs in both black and white and in colour have been selected by geographers in each member country. They have been chosen for their usefulness to the teacher of geography and salient geographical features have been underlined in accompanying legends.

It should be made clear from the outset that each of the following essays is the individual contribution of a geographer from the country described. Not only is it individual, but it is written to conform to no prescribed pattern of either content or presentation. Thus, some contributions are set out simply in note form to provide, for the teacher, those features of the country's geography which the contributors hope will be taught to pupils in other lands, while

---

[1] *Geography Teaching and the Revision of Geography Textbooks and Atlases.*

others take the form of carefully argued essays to challenge the thinking of the teacher and to provide ideas and material which he will distil at his discretion for use in the classroom. All, in fact, are different—and therein lies one of their merits; for one can gain from them not only up-to-date information about a country but perhaps also something of the way at least one of its geographers looks at the nature of geography and at its teaching in schools.

Also bound up with these essays is the chapter "Europe and its Regions" from *Geography Teaching and the Revision of Geography Textbooks*, Chapter II. This is included in order to keep the other perspective also in view—the concept of a Europe which is not merely the accumulation of its little national parts. In the English edition this chapter is taken straight from the original publication, as drafted by Professor East. The French edition makes use of a translation by Monsieur François which gives a free and interesting rendering of the original.

It remains only to offer sincere thanks to all the contributors. They have taken much trouble to ensure that their contributions measured up to their own high standards; some have entirely rewritten first drafts to reduce length to what was feasible in the present volume.

Thanks are also due to Monsieur Louis François who, by reason of his exciting *exposé* of the geography of France at the conference at Bray (1963), virtually initiated the idea—and who has now contributed a short but stimulating introduction.

Finally, our sincere thanks must go to Mr E. C. Marchant, formerly Her Majesty's Staff Inspector for Geography, co-ordinator of the Committee for General and Technical Education in the field of geography, who so thoroughly compiled and edited the text.

Contents

Introduction

The Council of Europe called upon geographers—authorities on the science of geography and its teaching methods—to present the geography of those European countries which had participated in earlier conferences on problems of the revision of textbooks and atlases. The book is equally suited to the cultured man who desires to know Europe better and to teachers and pupils who are studying our continent.

Each country is presented as seen through the eyes of one of its own geographers, but the work does not consist of a series of nationalistic panegyrics. The Council of Europe was anxious to produce a scientific and educational, but at the same time artistic, work presenting each country in a vivid and agreeable way. Europe has many countries, which are all, in their different ways, beautiful and varied, active and prosperous, and of which their citizens may be justly proud. But this book is intended, above all, to show that the old Europe, possessor of so great a past, is still very much alive, and even seems to have recovered fresh youth and vitality. Nations, which are made up of our individual lives, have a different existence from our own. They may, it is true, be young, then adult, then old, but they can also escape death and begin a new life-cycle as the result either of a heroic endeavour or of the ceaseless striving of their citizens. The same is true of Europe, insofar as the countries constituting it banish hostility while maintaining rivalry, concert their efforts, co-operate, and create an original community which will make this group of nations one of the great powers of the modern world.

There is no need to distort geography or make use of it in a particular way in order to promote a better understanding between nations and help preserve peace. It is sufficient that it should remain wholly itself and that it should be presented integrally, intelligently, and honestly. That truth is demonstrated once again by this book.

Europe and its Regions

INTRODUCTION

Europe is less defined by the oceans than are the other continents; indeed it is a western, peninsular extension of Asia which, as Count Alexander von Humboldt thought, is related to Asia rather as the peninsula of Brittany is related to the rest of France; it is comparable, too, in this respect with that south-eastern marginal land known to geographers as Monsoon Asia. The term 'Europe' is used nowadays very loosely and variously to refer to several parts of the continent as geographers have conventionally delimited it. Moreover, there has been some relatively minor disagreement among geographers themselves during the last two hundred years as to its precise eastern limits. For the ancient Greeks, who originated the concept 'Europe', these eastern limits were set either along the Caucasian river Rion or along the lower Don and the eastern shore of the Azov Sea. Modern geographers extend Europe's limits eastwards to a line along the eastern foot of the Ural mountains, along the Emba river, and along the Manych depression which extends from the lower Don towards the Caspian Sea; in this way, the whole of the Great Russian Lowlands is thus contained in Europe[1]. The Conferences recognized, however, the geographical unreality of these eastern limits.

Europe extends northwards to the Arctic Ocean, within which it includes many island groups, and north-westwards to include Iceland and a number of archipelagos. Greenland, though culturally and politically European, is now more fittingly regarded as part of North America. Geographers have long noted that the coastlands of the Mediterranean basin share common features of physical geography and, in a lesser degree, those of human geography. Even so, the Mediterranean is taken to divide off Europe from Africa, although its islands, including Cyprus, which is geologically a sundered part of Asia Minor, are grouped with Europe, as is also Asia

---

[1] Humboldt noted that, north of lat. 48°N., Europe and Asia melted into each other in wide plains or steppes and recalled that Herodotus was willing to include the Scythian steppe (now part of Western Siberia and Kazakhstan) in Europe: *Cosmos*, 7th ed. 1849, II, 137. A modern geographer included the West Siberian Lowlands. (H. Louis, "Über den geographischen Europabegriff", *Mitteilungen der Geographischen Gesellschaft in München;* Volume XXXIX, 1954, pp. 73–93.)

Minor, which makes up the greater part of Turkey. While conventionally Europe is said to end at the narrow waters of the Dardanelles-Sea of Marmara-Bosporus, thus bisecting Turkey, it is now sometimes thought that in certain contexts Europe may be held to take in the whole of this country whose economic and political interests are often more closely linked with the rest of Europe than with the countries of Afro-Asia. The continental frontier is, in fact, not a clear-cut one. To the west and south-west Europe has outliers in the Spanish Canary Islands and in the Portuguese Azores, Madeira, and Cape Verde Islands. Finally, although its commercial and Commonwealth interests are world-wide, there can be no doubt that the United Kingdom is geographically part of Europe.

The location of Europe near to the early cradles of civilization in the Near East favoured the spread into it in prehistoric times of civilized ways of life. It found itself centrally placed in the northern (land) hemisphere in modern times when the Atlantic Ocean was no longer a barrier on its western flank. Modern airways merely confirm this centrality.

Although a substantial fraction of Europe's territory lies north of lat. 60°, and even extends beyond the Arctic Circle, the bulk of it lies between lat. 60° and 35° in temperate latitudes. Thanks to its position on the western side of the Eurasian landmass and to its peninsular configuration, Europe enjoys for its latitudes a markedly favourable climate, its arid and polar areas being proportionately small. Other favourable facts are the surface waters of the Atlantic Ocean, which warm up the maritime air masses coming from the west, and the considerable extent of continental shelves, the latter providing not only fishing grounds but a source of fuel and energy resources from beneath the sea floor. Further, Europe's lands are so disposed that maritime navigation can penetrate deeply—for more than 3200 km. by way of the Mediterranean and Black Seas, and for about 1600 km. by way of the North and Baltic Seas.

The surface of Europe is made up of rocks of all ages and presents great variety of altitudes, relief, and landscapes. Prominent structural features are the Fennoscandian shield in the north, and the East European (Sarmatian) platform in the east, remnant Hercynian massifs, and mountain systems of the Alpine orogeny. Lowlands are relatively extensive, stretching eastwards from Ireland to broaden considerably where the continent is broadest between the Baltic and White Seas and the Black and Caspian Seas. Related to the Alpine mountain systems are also circumadjacent lowlands—in south-west France, north Italy, astride the middle and lower Danube, and in north Caucasus; so also submerged areas, such as the Adriatic and Aegean Seas. Although the continent became extensively wooded in post-glacial times, most of the woodland, outside northern Russia and Fennoscandinavia, has been cleared for agricultural use, since the cover of soils, many of which overlie glacial deposits, has proved well adapted to cultivation. Only in the interiors of Iberia and Anatolia, as also in the extreme south-east of European USSR, do dry steppe conditions necessitate irrigation for stability of production.

A striking feature of the physical geography of Europe is the way in which its surface is divided into compartments of different scale, smaller and more numerous towards the west. To this is related a no less remarkably diversified human geography which results from a long and continuous history of colonization and land-use. The peoples of Europe today present themselves less as a common type which can be labelled 'European' than as an assemblage of national groups distinguishable not only by nationality but also by language, historical traditions, territorial attachments, levels of material culture, and religious and ideological affiliations. Most of Europe's languages fall within the Indo-European family—notably those which are included in the Romance, Germanic, and Slavic groups—but many other languages are spoken both within and outside this main family. And to linguistic divisions are added those produced by the development in turn of many distinct nations and many national states, since increasingly national groups, fired by strong self-consciousness and purpose, have sought and obtained independent statehood. In this respect Europe appears today more divided than it was in 1913 when a number of large multi-national empires still organized the many nationalities of the greater part of the continent. Today few such markedly multi-national states exist in Europe apart from the federally organized USSR and Yugoslavia. As the German philosopher Count H. Keyserling wrote (in 1928): "We are dealing, in the case of Europe, with an outstandingly manifold, astoundingly riven structure; the Balkans constitute its truest prototype." Yet he added: "All Europe is essentially of one spirit", and "For me another premise is also the unity of Europe today."

Further on, the attempt is made to express verbally the nature and strength of European unity, elusive and imponderable though this may appear. Perhaps, looked at from outside, Europe, given its highly skilled and numerous population and its economic and commercial stature, may appear more clearly a unit than it does to its own inhabitants. Such unity as its inhabitants recognize depends much on the legacy of the past, though this varied regionally, as when certain peoples derived civilizing influences from Greece, Rome, Constantinople, or Baghdad. Much, too, depends on the effects of long sequences of war, in some of which Europeans co-operated against a common enemy or, more often, battled with each other. In modern and recent times Europe played its world role in the opening up of new lands—in the Americas, in Siberia and Kazakhstan, in South Africa and Australasia—to colonization and commerce. Today it is coming to share more uniformly than ever before the same features and the same effects of industrialization, based on scientific knowledge, capital investment, and technological achievement. Even though in its strivings to create larger units than the outworn nation-state it appears to create new divisions—as between the Six of the Common Market and the Seven of EFTA or as between the countries of NATO and those of the Warsaw Pact Organization—it is, in fact, treading a path, rough and tortuous, towards a unity which may in time give outward expression to the inner promptings of its peoples to recognize the geographical reality that history has created.

Such underlying unity as Europe may fittingly claim cannot conceal those striking regional and even local varieties of its physical and human geography which are mirrored on its surface. With these much in mind, the first Conference concluded that only by applying the methods of regional analysis was it possible to make clear in geography textbooks and in teaching the complex geography of the Continent as a whole. The same Conference believed that a division of Europe into five major units was both valid academically and desirable pedagogically. The case for a division into six units, by the addition of one named Danubian Central Europe, was discussed but rejected. Accordingly, the first Conference turned to the consideration of Central Europe, leaving to later meetings that of the other four.

One of the objectives and achievements of the series of Conferences, therefore, was to establish that each of these five major regions, in the light of geographical analysis, could be validly conceived. Thus in the sections which follow are presented brief and concise geographical justifications of these regions, to which are added indications of their territorial contents and limits. These last are conceived and expressed in both physical and political terms; the former, which are given as zonal frontiers, do not precisely coincide with the latter, which are the linear boundaries of states. The five regions are: Central Europe, Southern Europe, Western Europe, Northern Europe, and Eastern Europe. These names were agreed after some discussions; the regions were examined in this order, and are thus discussed below.

CENTRAL EUROPE

In August–September 1961 the first Conference met at Goslar and was confronted with the problem of 'Central Europe' in its geographical aspect. Its task in this respect was the hardest of all its tasks for two reasons: first because what it decided about Central Europe would affect its later work and second because the concept 'Central Europe' raised special difficulties to which it is necessary to refer.

These difficulties were essentially political and related to the present and the past. The term 'Central Europe' had long been used by geographers, but also by others, and the territorial meanings ascribed to it have been widely variant, some even grotesque. Certainly this concept was German in origin, certainly it had suffered acutely from use in frankly political contexts; even its use by many geographers could be shown to have had political undertones. In short, as *Mitteleuropa*, the term 'Central Europe' was a concept of politics, or at best, of either physical or political geography only, and it was thought mainly to apply to an expansionist area of German political interest. At the end of World War II, *Mitteleuropa* in this sense had clearly disappeared. What had been an indefinite area, of which Germany was the core, had vanished, leaving only a line—the Iron Curtain—*i.e.*, the boundaries between the Soviet-controlled territories of Eastern Germany, Czechoslovakia, and Austria on the one hand and the areas of Germany and Austria occupied by the Western Powers on the other. The Conference faced initially the problem whether in fact 'Central Europe' had any valid conceptual existence. The fact that Germany, under the Potsdam Agreements and pending the signature of a peace treaty, had been deprived of territories to the advantage of Poland and the USSR and had been partitioned into a western and eastern occupied zone, the fact that Berlin was itself divided into zones of military occupation, and, lastly, the existence of a division between the Federal Republic of Germany and the German Democratic Republic were necessarily much in the minds of the geographers at Goslar in 1961, although they were concerned with the academic question: did 'Central Europe' make sense as a major geographical region of Europe and, if so, on what basis did it rest, and what were its characteristics and its limits?

As a result of its discussions the Conference came firmly to the view that, as the following report explains, Central Europe fittingly takes its place among the major regions of the continent.

On the ground of location alone, one major part of Europe is so distinguishable from the others as to deserve a designation such as 'Central', 'Middle', or even 'Interior' Europe. It is that inner, isthmian, and intermediate area of the continent which was called *Zwischeneuropa* on a Haack wall map of the inter-war period. This area separates markedly peninsular and insular lands to the west, north, and south from those more markedly 'continental' to the east, above all in European USSR: these last, in scale, in climate, as also in some of their historical relationships, show north Asian characteristics. Central Europe, thus broadly defined by location, links the North and Baltic Seas with the Mediterranean world and links also European lands to the west and east. It fulfils within Europe an essential cross-road function and has done this from prehistoric times, when Neolithic colonists cleared by fire the woodlands of many areas, notably those where loess deposits occurred, for farming and for circulation. Consideration of the facts of physical, historical, and human geography makes it possible to give more reality than this to the concept 'Central Europe' — this term was preferred—and even to attempt its delimitation.

Other aspects of physical geography, besides location, provide criteria for defining Central Europe: these are certain effects of geological history, relief, and climate. In Central Europe all of three contrasted physical environments are found: mountains of the Alpine orogeny, Hercynian massifs, and the lowlands of glacial deposition in the north. In this part of Europe the Hercynian massifs are more broken up by faults and more divided into blocks and associated depressions than elsewhere in Europe. In this part of Europe, further, maritime and continental influences of climate meet in a pendulum movement. In turn maritime influences move towards the east and continental influences extend towards the west. The latter are marked above all by the freezing of the rivers in winter and by maximum precipitation in summer. The climate, moreover, is modified locally by the relief so that the Hercynian massifs receive a more abundant precipitation than the lowlands; in contrast, the basins and the depressions are relatively dry and warmer in summer. A marked contrast exists between the landscapes of the massifs and the lowlands not only in climate, but also in soils and land use: the former being wooded, the latter cultivated. In short, Central Europe can be envisaged as an area of associated physical landscapes across which one passes from the maritime to the continental type of climate, or vice versa.

From the standpoint of historical geography, Central Europe is that part of Europe on which, as a result of its geographical position and configuration, many very different peoples have converged and within which they settled. Among the most important groups are the Germans, the West Slavs (Poles, Czechs, and Slovaks), the Magyars, the Romanians, and others. Central Europe not only attracted invaders but was also a source of immigrants to other neighbouring parts of Europe. These movements of people, and the existence of small natural compartments of the land, help to explain the complexity of its history and political geography. An outstanding theme of its history focuses on the two most important groups — the Germans and the Slavs. These meet each other in Central Europe and throughout history have been either associated or in opposition. Further, it should be noted that cultural influences from the west, east, north, and south have converged on Central Europe and have entered into the original cultural traits which it presents.

Another characteristic feature of Central Europe is the many large towns, the surviving churches, town halls, and palaces, which bear architectural witness to their vitality and wealth during the later Middle Ages and the Renaissance. Most of these originated and grew from the tenth century onwards, being the result of German colonization eastwards, and their flowering reflected the commercial activity, the power of the Church, and the splendour of the imperial monarchy. Many became veritable city states ('Free Cities'), and Central Europe presented a truly urban civilization. The siting and distribution of these towns provide a commentary on the thoroughfare character of Central Europe noted above: some north of the Alps occupy crossroad sites where trade routes from Alpine passes converge; others have a similar cross-road function in relation to routes passing through and north of the Hercynian massifs; yet another 'line' of towns is situated on or near the coast of the North and Baltic Seas, and these were organized for trade inland and seawards by the Hanseatic League.

Central Europe and, above all, the Federal Republic of Germany are characterized by an economy in which industrial and commercial activity are outstanding. Industrialization is largely the result of the last hundred years, or indeed less, and a policy of industrial development is pursued vigorously everywhere. Most notable among a wide range of industries are those which produce iron and steel, machine tools, chemicals (including petro-chemicals), transport equipment, and textiles. Although manufacturing is widely spread, it shows marked concentration—in the large cities, such as Hamburg, Berlin, Prague, Warsaw, Zürich, Vienna, and Budapest, and in areas of major if differing scale. North Rhine-Westphalia contains great metallurgical, chemical, textile, and other industries and a conurbation, both of which are sustained by the Ruhr coalfield; the German Democratic Republic bases industries on its considerable resources of brown coal; and Poland now commands practically the whole of the Upper Silesian coalfield and its industrial towns. Other sources of fuel and energy are increasingly provided by piped petroleum, to supplement modest local resources, either from the seaports or from the USSR, and by hydro-electricity, especially in Switzerland and Austria; these clearly permit a wider geographical distribution of industry as they much lessen former dependence on coal. Other factors which contribute to the high degree of industrialization of Central Europe are large-scale capital investment, the results of intensive scientific research, technological advances, and, over much of the area, the availability of highly skilled labour forces which, in the Federal Republic of Germany, were supplemented by numerous immigrant workers. And although there are distinctions to be drawn between the industrial and commercial activities of the 'Western' and 'Communist' countries—e.g., in their commercial affiliations, the direction of their trade, and the ways in which industry is organized—they share the common trend towards industrial growth and urbanization.

Lastly, it is notable that Central Europe lacks political unity; indeed political and territorial instability has characterized its history. The events following World War II have left it divided economically and politically. Clearly geographical and historical factors explain this situation.

The Limits of Central Europe and Recommendations

The Conference recommended that, in order not to complicate the study of the geography of Europe and to facilitate its teaching and understanding, the continent should be divided into five major regions, not more.

The limits of Central Europe are given in both physical and political terms. These limits are not co-terminous; moreover, those of the former have the character of frontier zones, whereas those of the latter, being political boundaries, are linear. It was agreed that in the geography of Europe attention must be paid to nations, as fundamental and restricting realities, no less than to the physical features of the environment.

In physical geography the limits of Central Europe are found, to the north, along the coasts of the North and Baltic Seas, except that Denmark is more fittingly grouped with Northern Europe (*q.v.*) and the Low Countries are assigned to Western Europe. To the south Central Europe extends to the central and eastern Alps and, beyond the Pannonian lowland, to the first ranges of the Dinaric Alps. To the west the Rhineland and the crests of the Jura and the Alps mark the limit of Central Europe, while eastwards its limits may be taken along the Niemen, beyond which the Baltic Heights disappear, and along the upper Vistula and San, beyond which Hercynian massifs cease to reach the surface.

The countries which lie either wholly in Central Europe or have the greater part of their territory there and thus should be studied within this framework are: the Federal Republic of Germany, the German Democratic Republic, Poland, Switzerland, Austria, Czechoslovakia, and Hungary. The Conference considered, but decided not to include, Yugoslavia, because it is in part a Balkan and also a Mediterranean country (see section below on Southern Europe). Further, after discussion, it left for later consideration the regional allocation of Romania.

SOUTHERN EUROPE

Although the term 'Mediterranean' fittingly applies to much of the greater part of southern Europe which lies within this sea and shares a climate which bears its name, the term 'Southern Europe' is preferred, since this can be used to include adjacent countries— Portugal, Northern Spain, and Bulgaria — which have no Mediterranean coasts.

Southern Europe fronts the Atlantic Ocean to the west and the Black Sea to the east, but largely projects into the Mediterranean basin, thus bringing Europe into close proximity to Africa and Asia.

Its peninsulas narrow the entries to the Mediterranean Sea, which extends longitudinally for over 3500 km., at the Atlantic and Black Sea approaches, and also divide its basin into a number of semi-enclosed seas—the Tyrrhenian, Adriatic, Ionian, and Aegean—which all contain island groups. Winds, islands, and surface currents all played their part in the development of Mediterranean navigation, but the sea, being deep and poorly endowed with continental shelves, has relatively little value for fisheries. The extent, shape, and location of the Mediterranean—between lat. 45° and about 32°N.—are important in relation both to climate and to commerce. Its importance to commerce is the more evident when it is recalled that its waterway is prolonged into the Azov and Black Seas (where Southern Europe makes contact with Eastern Europe) and via the Suez Canal into the Red Sea, by which route Europe makes contact with Monsoon Asia.

Although the Mediterranean type of climate is widely character-istic of Southern Europe, especially of its coastlands, it is not the only climate experienced there. The climate is continental rather than Mediterranean in the North Italian Plain and in the interior lowlands of Yugoslavia and Bulgaria, and it is oceanic rather than Mediterranean in the north of Portugal and Spain. Further, the Mediterranean climate is markedly modified by altitude inland from the coasts.

Southern Europe owes this climate to the fact that it lies between, and thus in contact with, two major air masses; to the south the source region of tropical air masses, and to the north the source region of polar air masses. As a result of the seasonal latitudinal displacement of these air masses, the temperate oceanic climate extends over the Mediterranean world from mid-September to late May. From the end of May to mid-September desert-type character-istics predominate especially during summer. The combination of heat and dryness during these months normally hinders plant growth. Rainfall is irregularly distributed throughout the year, with a pronounced droughty season in summer. But rainfall is likewise irregular from year to year, to a degree that shows marked variations from the average. The efficiency of the rainfall is further reduced in many areas by extensive limestone outcrops.

To these irregularities in climate must be added irregularities in its geographical distribution; generously watered areas contrast with arid ones. These contrasts are mainly due to the effects of exposure and orography. Another notable feature of the Mediterranean climate is the violent intrusion of local cold winds such as the *mistral* and the *bora*. These drainage winds are fed by anticyclonic polar air to the north and are associated with the passage of depressions. Such winds have a drying effect which is sometimes catastrophic to vegetation. The xerophytic aspect of the vegetation illustrates the regular occurrence of long summer drought; the forest is widely replaced by *maquis* or *garrigue*. And the hazards of this special climate have to be faced in agriculture calling for special farming methods.

Southern Europe is characterized also by the juxtaposition of lowlands and high relief which gives rise to marked local contrasts. Everywhere mountains confront seas and plains. These mountains consist of Alpine ranges, such as those which form the northern borderlands of this part of Europe, and those which project into the Balearic Islands, Sicily, and Crete; or again, they may be massifs broken and up-thrust by the repercussions of the Alpine orogeny. These mountains rise boldly above either small alluvial or deltaic plains or large basins of subsidence within massifs or chains such as the plains of Andalusia, Aragon, the Po, the lower Danube, and the Maritza. Owing to its relief the landscape of Southern Europe gives a general impression of subdivision and discontinuity.

The mountainous ramparts in the north are breached by routeways of varying importance. The widest and most important is the one leading either towards the Atlantic by the Carcassonne Gap or towards Western and Central Europe via the Rhône corridor. At the head of the Adriatic the mountain barrier is narrower and lower, thus affording fairly easy approaches to the middle Danubian basin. So also north of the Aegean, the Vardar (Axios) valley leads either to that of the Morava and the Belgrade region or else to the basin of Sofia, and thence to Istanbul or to the Isker valley, which leads in turn to the Bucharest region. Finally, maritime routes to and from Southern Europe are provided in the east by the straits of the Dardanelles and the Bosporus and in the west by the Strait of Gibraltar.

The direction of the mountain arcs makes it possible to distinguish a western and an eastern basin in the Mediterranean, with peninsular Italy and Sicily at the junction of the two. To the west there are smooth coastlines and massive islands, to the east extremely indented coasts and (apart from Cyprus and Crete) archipelagos of small islands. This division into two basins, western and eastern, holds good for climate as well, since the contrasts between the wet and dry sides of high ground and of coasts becomes more marked towards the east and the eastern basin is located farther south.

The rugged mountains are subject to irregular but violent rains, which cause severe erosion and the accumulation of masses of detritus in the lowlands. The water-courses are generally torrential and unnavigable and build up deltas near their mouths. The erosion of the soil from the slopes, facilitated by centuries of forest clearance for timber, results in the deposition of steep alluvial cones, projecting into and thus restricting farming in the valley bottoms and on the plains. Where the lowlands are bounded inland by these fans and seawards by sandspits, marshes are found (in Italian *maremme*). Certainly Southern Europe is a region of sea and high insolation, which always attracted man, but its other physical conditions make human occupance difficult. Only by unremitting effort has man been able to win, and above all to hold, his conquest.

It is not surprising that Southern Europe cradled the first European civilizations, since Europeans in the eastern Mediterranean came into contact with the earlier centres of civilized life in the Near East. In classical antiquity civilization, developed from earlier prehistoric beginnings, expressed itself in the life of city states with their fortified cities sited in plains, mountain-girt and cultivated, with access to the sea. Civilization flourished successively in Greece and Latium, spreading widely from these two, since Byzantium (as Constantinople) and Rome became the centres of expanding Christendom. The spiritual and cultural vitality of Southern Europe was later enriched by contacts with Arabic civilization; there followed also the Italian Renaissance, the Portuguese maritime discoveries, and the golden century of Spain. The whole of Europe shared the heritage bequeathed by Southern Europe.

In recent centuries this part of Europe lost its former ascendancy in step with the rise in the political and economic strength of Western and Central Europe; this was foreshadowed by the revolt from Rome —the Reformation—which released new energies and initiatives. The physical and political fragmentation of so much of Southern Europe, the exploitation by West European countries of the new maritime routes, and the loss of maritime ascendancy even in the Mediterranean itself—such factors as these contributed to Southern Europe's relative decline, which was most marked in the nineteenth and early twentieth centuries. Its economy appeared to stagnate, resting essentially on agriculture, much of which was for mere subsistence; and agriculture suffered alike from outmoded agrarian and social systems and from a remarkably unstable physical setting where soil was lost by erosion, marshes extended, aridity imposed real difficulties, and intricate terracing of hill slopes was often a prerequisite for cultivation. For a variety of reasons Southern Europe was not able to join early in modern industrialization and, accordingly, as its population grew during the nineteenth century, sheer poverty stimulated migration, above all to the Americas. However, recent decades have witnessed a remarkable renewal of political and social vigour in Southern Europe, both in countries where State planning is being applied to the economy (Yugoslavia, Bulgaria, and Albania) and in those where the State co-ordinates new developments (e.g., Italy and Turkey).

Since it lacked large deposits of coal and of iron, Southern Europe was at a serious disadvantage in the early days of modern industrialism. However, in certain other respects it has been favoured. The opening of the Suez Canal in 1869 improved the geographical position of the Mediterranean countries. The railway and the steamship facilitated the export of agricultural produce to wider markets: olive oil, citrus, and other fruits, vegetables, flowers, and wine. With the ever-widening discovery and use of petroleum, these countries find themselves well placed to import supplies cheaply by sea from a variety of sources in South-West Asia, North Africa (which offers also natural gas), and Eastern Europe (European USSR). The exploitation of certain minerals has proved commercially rewarding: bauxite in Yugoslavia and Italy; copper in Spain; sulphur in Sicily; chrome in Turkey, while deposits of modest or small scale are regionally valuable: such are coal in Turkey, iron ore in Italy, Spain, and Turkey. Metallurgical industries have been built up—e.g., aluminium in Yugoslavia and Italy; steel, notably in Italy, but also elsewhere. Italy, Greece, and Spain command large merchant fleets. And it should not be forgotten that Southern Europe has at its disposal a large growing labour force on which economic progress depends; the increase is 0·8 % per year[1], a figure still somewhat reduced by net emigration, and the levels of skill fall far short of those, for example, of Northern Europe. The continuing advances in science and technology make increasingly possible more effective measures to improve agriculture and to harness an unstable environment to human use: by controlling floods, draining marshes,

---

[1] The crude death rates of the countries of Southern Europe conform with those of Europe generally, although the infantile mortality remains high.

irrigation works, the adoption of scientific crop rotations, refforestation, and the generation of hydro-electric energy. This last, where sufficiently developed, has fostered substantial textile, metallurgical, and chemical industries, especially in northern Italy and northeast Spain. The use of solar and nuclear energy will offer new opportunities to populous areas as yet ill favoured for industrial activity.

The use of the Mediterranean as an east-west highway of commerce is so evident as possibly to overshadow the strong north-south (and south-north) movements which now join Southern Europe to the rest of the continent to the north. Along this line exports and re-exports (especially of petroleum) pass northwards, as do workers seeking agricultural and factory employment; from north to south come coal from the Ruhr, manufactures, and an ever-increasing flow of tourists bringing valuable foreign exchange. This association between Southern Europe and the other parts of the continent, which is beneficial to the whole, is attested by the operations of the Common Market of which Italy is a founder member and Greece and Turkey are associates (there are many associates, too, in Africa). It is attested also by Bulgaria's membership of COMECON, and by the trade which now takes place between the USSR and South European countries—e.g., Italy and Turkey.

Southern Europe then should no longer be envisaged as a region of sunlit backwardness or as a museum piece. Low living standards indeed persist and educational standards are not everywhere adequate to an age of opportunity and rapid change. The remarkable industrial revival of post-1945 Italy, which makes her one of the leading industrial countries of Europe, coupled with continuing developments in Turkey, Yugoslavia, and elsewhere, suggest afresh the potentialities for material progress which Southern Europe possesses. And as background to these dynamic changes, note should be taken of the external help and stimulus which have come from the United States through its financial aid and its commercial activities—e.g., cheap seaborne coal to Italy.

Delimitation of Southern Europe and Recommendations

The physical limits of Southern Europe are largely provided by its Atlantic, Mediterranean, and Black Sea shores. To the north they may be found in the mountainous areas of northern Spain, the Cevennes, Alps, Dinaric Alps, and the Balkan range. In the east Southern Europe extends inland from the sea coasts of Asia Minor to merge, and overlap with, South-West Asia.

Southern Europe comprises Mediterranean countries and some others with territories lying wholly or partially beyond the Mediterranean: Portugal and Spain in the Iberian Peninsula, Italy, Yugoslavia, Albania, Bulgaria, Greece, and Turkey. In addition, Cyprus and Malta, as newly independent states, fall within this region, as do also the microstates of Monaco, San Marino, the Papal State, Andorra, and the Crown colony of Gibraltar. The Canary Islands of Overseas Spain and the Madeiras and Azores of Overseas Portugal are fittingly to be regarded as cultural outliers of Southern Europe.

It is recommended that the Mediterranean Midi of France should be studied as part of France within the framework of Western Europe. It is further recommended that the geography of Turkey should be studied as a whole, as part of both Southern Europe and South-West (or West) Asia. The latter recommendation takes account not only of Turkey's formally European territory near to the Turkish Straits so-called, and of its affinities with Southern Europe in respect of location, climate, and geological structure, but also of its close relationship with Europe as a whole, which is illustrated by its membership of NATO and the Council of Europe and its associate membership of EEC. Lastly, there are some grounds for studying Romania as part of Southern Europe.

WESTERN EUROPE

Western Europe is that part of the continent where the co-existence of land and tidal sea has proved most advantageous. Like Northern Europe and Southern Europe, between which it lies, it confronts the Atlantic Ocean and, like the former, it can be distinguished by reference to the continental shelf which either surrounds or borders its coasts. This shelf extends from south-west France, around Ireland and Britain, and across the North Sea. The lands of Western Europe, which rise—in a few places precariously—above the shallow waters of this shelf, present a distinctive configuration in that they are broken up (but not decimated) into islands (major and minor) and peninsulas, washed by the tidal waters of inland seas (the North Sea and Irish Sea) and of many straits, such as the English Channel and St George's Channel. The area of Western Europe, since it coincides with the narrowing oceanic extremity of the continent, is necessarily reduced, so that it is the smallest of the five major regions of Europe. However, its size has not detracted from its potentialities, and its peripheral location, projected towards North America, has proved as favourable in modern times as it was remote and ill favoured in prehistory when the Atlantic and Arctic oceans framed Europe rigidly to the west and north.

The shelf is a former continental expanse which was partially flooded by the sea waters of the Flandrian transgression. This submerged portion of the continent, with waters less than (in places very much less than) 200 m. deep, contains fishing grounds which still play an important role in the economic life of Europe, and now promises energy supplies in the form of petroleum and natural gas. From the sea estuaries penetrate deeply into the land, thus providing facilities for trade, the more so since the tides help to carry ships far upstream. In some parts, especially along the coast of the Netherlands, the very low range of the tides, as a result of the convergence of opposed tidal currents, has facilitated land reclamation and the creation of polders and made it possible to build ports like Rotterdam without the need for locks.

The landforms of Western Europe, except for those of south-eastern and southern France which belong to the Alpine mountain system, are relatively subdued yet greatly varied. They are relatively subdued because the fold systems, which created the region by their formation in the north and south respectively, are ancient, being of Caledonian and Hercynian age. Tectonic forces, which broke up the primary rocks into sedimentary basins and massifs, were responsible for the variety of features, further accentuated by the varying intensity of the tectonic forces from one place to another. Maximum intensity occurred in the north and south of the region as a result of the increased crustal movements in the north-east Atlantic and the Alps. There resulted somewhat sharp contrasts between highlands and lowlands in Scotland, Ireland, and Wales on the one hand and the Massif Central on the other, large-scale fractures being accompanied by volcanic eruptions. In contrast, the central part of Western Europe consists of the Anglo-Flemish and Paris basins, which are inter-connected by sills across low hills. The geological and morphological evolution of Western Europe has created a wide variety of terrains and soils: low-lying plains and enclosed basins of clay, marl, and sand, the basin bordered by scarplands of chalk, limestone, and sandstone: siliceous soils on the surfaces of old massifs, peat-bogs in badly drained low-lying ground or on high, old, ill-drained surfaces. And it should be noted that the Quaternary glaciation left behind more clay drift than sand and gravel north of a line from Cork to

Nijmegen; on the landscape the depositional rather than the erosional features of glaciation are the more significant.

The climate of Western Europe, 'oceanic' in type, is determined by its latitude and by its situation on the eastern shores of the Atlantic Ocean. The region is almost constantly exposed to the influences of moisture-carrying air masses moving from the west and to depressions travelling east along the polar front, where air masses of various origins and natures—arctic, polar maritime, and tropical maritime—are in constant interaction. Cold, dry air of either polar continental or arctic origin sometimes reaches this region in winter, whilst tropical air masses in the form of anticyclones, travelling north from the Azores, bring fine summer weather. The recurrent cycle of variable weather acts as a reassuring and stabilizing factor in agriculture. Rainfall is always adequate (600–800 mm.) in the lowlands and abundant on high ground with westerly exposure. Rain usually falls with moderate intensity; the heaviest falls occur in the cold season, but there is no lack of rain in summer.

The flow of air from the sea keeps temperatures within a moderate range and without violent extremes, and the intermediate seasons are consequently late and prolonged. At sea-level temperatures range between 2° and 8°C. in the coldest month and between 12° and 22°C. in the warmest month. Frost is rare on the western coasts but becomes increasingly frequent as one moves east. It is in winter that the influence of the sea is most marked and favourable, as is shown by the roughly meridional direction of the isotherms. In addition, the Atlantic drift brings relatively warm surface water to all coasts, thereby ensuring, even as far north as northern Scotland, winters such as latitude alone could not sufficiently explain.

In spite of the homogeneity of this climate, important regional variations are discernible. The western areas are most obviously influenced by the sea and suffer considerable cloudiness. Towards the east, on the inland borders of the Benelux countries and of France, certain characteristics foreshadow the climate of Central Europe: high temperatures and more sunshine in summer, lower total rainfall and a gradual change to maximum rainfall in summer. The influence of relief and altitude should also be noted: they account for high rainfall (e.g., on the windward mountain slopes) and they lower temperatures and reduce vegetation near the coast. While almost everywhere inland there is a cover of vegetation and rural settlements, these cease at a much lower altitude along the seaward fringes.

Patterns of vegetation in Western Europe are strongly influenced by these climatic conditions. On the one hand, almost everywhere there is luxuriant vegetation which contrasts with the stark aspect of the seaward fringe areas. This richness is apparent in the greenness of the plant cover, but derives also from the fact that plants from adjacent regions find a ready welcome in this area despite insular factors which tend to limit migration and to increase the endemic character of vegetation. Thus, for example, certain Mediterranean species have travelled along the Atlantic coast, crossed the Landes of Gascony and west Brittany, and even reached south-western Ireland; or they may have survived in these places as relics of a warmer age. Richness and variety are encouraged by the equable thermal conditions and by the abundant, but not excessive, moisture. On the other hand, the vegetation cover may appear somewhat thin as a result of the predominance of low growths—on grassland, moor, and scrubland—over forest which dwindles and thins out as one moves from Central Europe towards the Atlantic. This is due in part to natural conditions: the low summer temperatures and the force and salinity of winds striking islands and exposed peninsulas; but also to the cover of acid soil on the ancient massifs, although these are much lower than those of Central Europe. These factors are responsible for the low altitude and precariousness of the vegetation. But it is also an undoubted fact that early prolonged and intensive human activity made serious inroads into the forests. Re-afforestation projects recently undertaken have been very successful in the innermost parts of Western Europe, but have a somewhat uncertain hold along the promontories of the Atlantic coast.

One of the marked characteristics of Western Europe is its intense seafaring activity, evidenced by the large number of fishing ports and of fishing fleets which operate on the banks of the North Sea and on the continental shelf where it extends into the Atlantic and towards the Arctic Ocean. Other signs are the trading ports sited either along the coasts or at the heads or the mouths of estuaries. These are especially numerous and important on the coasts of the English Channel and the North Sea. The network of sea routes opens out in all directions over the Atlantic Ocean, but there are also sea routes linking up with Baltic countries. A dense network of roads, railways, and waterways relates these ports to populous and well-developed hinterlands. Finally, in Western Europe lies one of the outstanding focal points for airways, a fact which demonstrates the ever-important international role of its component countries.

The airports of London and Paris are among the busiest in the world.

Four of the nations of Western Europe were major colonial Powers, spreading western civilization and its methods of economic development throughout the world. Moreover, these countries continue to maintain close relations with the states which have emerged from their former colonies, retaining with them not only cultural links but also some degree of monetary, economic, and political association.

Western Europe plays an outstanding part in world trade. Indeed, this was the decisive factor in the accumulation of capital, which, while considerable at the beginning of modern times, has appreciably increased since the beginning of the nineteenth century. The investment of this capital, along with successive inventions, made possible the development of large-scale industries. Deposits of coal and iron ore, previously exploited on a small scale, formed the basis of a powerful and diversified metallurgical industry, whilst the use of machines, in turn driven by water and steam power, revolutionized the textile industry which came to use new materials obtained by trading, and more recently, an increasing range of home-produced synthetic fibres. Although coal remains the chief source of power, it is yielding to the competition of mineral oil, an ever-increasing amount of which has to be imported despite recent local discoveries of natural gas, which, too, is imported. The first refineries to be built, far from the sources of supply but close to the immediate consumers, were those of Western Europe. Finally, hydro-electric plants have been built (notably in France) to supplement the production of thermal electricity, while the generation of nuclear-electrical energy has been achieved.

Vast quantities of ore, including iron ore, and all types of raw materials are imported to contribute to the expansion of large-scale heavy industries as well as the production of manufactured goods, especially in the field of mechanical and electrical construction.

The development of industry and trade from the Middle Ages onwards resulted in greater power accruing to the middle classes in the towns. Industrial and commercial expansion since the Industrial Revolution has added to the political power of both middle and working classes and has led to the revival and spread of ideas of national independence, liberty, democracy, and respect for human rights. All the countries of Western Europe—itself the early home of the nation-state—have, at different times and for different

c

reasons, taken the lead in such movements. From the second half of the nineteenth century economic and social revolutionary ideas and endeavours went hand in hand with political change, itself often revolutionary in character.

The extraordinary growth of towns, fostered by the industrial and transport revolutions, has been fed by an inflow from the countryside and has led to a marked redistribution of population. Whereas industry employs more than half of the working population in the highly industrialized countries, the proportion of agricultural labour there falls as low as 6% (United Kingdom) and 7% (Belgium) (cf. France 20% and Ireland 42%).

Except in some areas of the ancient massifs on the Atlantic seaboard and inland, and except for the urbanized areas, the country is an almost uninterrupted expanse of farmland. There is a contrast between the hedged fields of Britain and Ireland on the one hand and the large open fields more characteristic across the English Channel, the latter being divided into small plots, medieval in origin, which still prevail despite recent and continuing efforts to consolidate them. Land clearance for cultivation continues—although land is lost continually to airfields and growing towns and suburbs—and at the same time work is undertaken to reclaim land subject to flooding by building dykes and by draining and exploiting peat bogs.

The characteristic type of farming in Western Europe is mixed farming—i.e., the cultivation of crops (in rotation) in conjunction with stock breeding and dairy farming. Indeed, in some regions first-class pioneer work has been done to eliminate fallow land, to cultivate industrial crops, and to introduce new systems of crop rotation.

In this part of Europe industry started, at an earlier stage than in most regions, to influence agriculture strongly by providing urban markets, by providing implements and fertilizers, and also by luring away part of the rural labour force. Similarly, the requirements of trade necessitated changes that were frequently of a radical nature. The advent first of Russian and then of American wheat supplies at the end of the nineteenth century caused wheat growing to yield place to stock breeding, the products of which were in immediate demand in the towns. The greater opportunities afforded by railway and steamship transport led to crop specialization aimed at high-quality products. This is what happened in the cases of market gardening linked to towns, and to industrial crop farming, dairy farming, and meat and bacon production. In fact, stock breeding is the branch which most benefits from such specialization: low mountain and the wetter lowlands have been turned into pasture and increasing use has been made of light soils for the cultivation of potatoes and fodder crops. In some alluvial areas fatstock breeding is combined with large-scale cultivation of crops. Stock breeding has become the main occupation of farmers in the countries of Western Europe and brings in up to four-fifths of their revenue.

Yet despite its resources and regionally high yields, its specialization and advanced farming methods, this part of Europe, with its large urban and industrial population, is not self-sufficient in food production. Indeed, it constitutes the greatest market in the world for imported agricultural produce, including animal foodstuffs needed for modern stock breeding and industrial fibres and oilseeds. Furthermore, specialized farming, like industrialization, has accentuated the contrast between the high- and low-lying land, between the Atlantic west and a wide eastern belt.

England, the Benelux countries, and northern France are densely populated areas where half or more of the working population is employed in industry, where farming is highly productive, and where the standard of living is high. In contrast, in Ireland, Wales, and Highland Scotland extend regions which have retained the system of family smallholdings devoted to mixed farming. Here there is still a certain degree of over-population in spite of relatively low population densities. Industry is sporadic, and in some instances its introduction was delayed by historical factors. And it is in the Atlantic outposts of Europe, Brittany included, that the Celtic languages have survived and that a strong outward movement of population has taken place.

Western Europe undoubtedly represents a unit of civilization and of technological progress, but has not yet achieved real unity. The United Kingdom and other countries in the north, centre, and even south of Europe are members of a trade association (EFTA), whilst France and the Benelux countries are united with the Federal Republic of Germany and Italy in a Common Market. This schism, the result of competition, is doubtless only a temporary one since economic ties between the United Kingdom and the continental countries are still strong, whilst everywhere there is apparent an industrial and commercial vitality which demands greater markets.

These western countries, which once exercised influence throughout the world by means of their colonial enterprises, might well have suffered decline following the emancipation of their vast dependencies and the great growth in the economic and political stature of the United States and the Soviet Union. This is far from being the case; the old metropolitan countries have adapted themselves to the new world order and have not only maintained but actually expanded their activities.

Delimitation of Western Europe and Recommendations

Western Europe is bordered by the Atlantic Ocean and the North Sea, and extends from the northern limits of the Mediterranean Midi of France and the Douro river northwards to include Scotland and its outlying islands. At its extreme limits it extends from Denmark and northern Scotland in the north, to the provinces of north-west Portugal (Minho) and of Spain (Galicia, Asturias, and the Basque province) in the south. However, it is recommended that Spain and Portugal should be studied within the framework of Southern Europe, Germany within that of Central Europe, the whole of France within that of Western Europe, and Denmark, together with Norway and Sweden, as part of Northern Europe.

Accordingly, the countries which form part of Western Europe and should be studied within this framework are: the United Kingdom, Ireland, France, Belgium, the Netherlands, and Luxembourg.

NORTHERN EUROPE

Northern Europe (or Norden) occupies only part of Europe's most northerly lands. These alternative terms for this major region apply to a group of peninsulas and islands, with coasts on the Atlantic and Arctic Oceans and on the North and the Baltic Seas, which stands north of Western and Central Europe and north-west of Eastern Europe.

Crossed by the Arctic Circle, Northern Europe is characterized by a climate less favourable than that of Western Europe, yet one which markedly benefits from the presence of the warm surface waters of the ocean. Cyclonic influences, which involve the passage over these lands of maritime air masses, play a preponderant part. The facts of location and climate help to explain that, although Norden was settled late as compared with the rest of the continent, it became earlier civilized than other parts of the world in comparable latitudes.

However, given the territorial scale of Norden and the altitudinal variations within it, climate shows clear regional differences. In particular, an oceanic and a Baltic type should be distinguished. The rainfall, in all seasons, along the western fringes (more than 2 m. a year and sometimes much more locally), is among the highest in Europe. The Maritime area is further characterized by cooler summers and more temperate winters, especially by the latter. The Baltic type is marked by continental features, such as cold winters, warmer summers, and lower precipitation figures, with maximum rainfall occurring in summer. In the Baltic area the study of temperature figures leads also to the distinction of a northern climatic zone which has much lower winter temperatures. This is reflected, for instance, in the freezing of the northern half of the Baltic Sea in winter.

Another marked characteristic of Northern Europe derives from the Quaternary glaciations, numerous traces of which, together with those of former marine transgressions, are frequently to be found in the landscape: U-shaped valleys, fjords, lakes, ill-graded water-courses (which provide sites for hydro-electric installations in the mountains), *roches moutonnées*, moraines, drumlins, eskers, and a variety of fluvio-glacial deposits in the plains. In Iceland, too, account should be taken of the extent of present glaciers. The Vatnajökull (8400 sq. km. in area) is the greatest glacier in Europe.

The landscape reflects also the variety of the underlying rocks. The Baltic Shield, the oldest part of Europe, may be considered the heart of the region, but to the west and south are different physical elements: a zone of Caledonian structures, the lowlands of Denmark and Skåne, with younger sedimentary formations; and the volcanic formations of Tertiary and Quaternary age in the Faroes and Iceland. It should be noted that the greater part of the coasts of Northern Europe, like those of Western Europe, are bordered by broad continental shelves which support valuable fisheries.

Climatic differences are reflected also in the soils and vegetation covers. To the west strong winds often discourage the growth of forest, even near sea-level, and grassland predominates: the pine penetrates farthest to the west (in Norway), but the spruce is not precluded by climate. The continental part of Northern Europe, where the summers are warmer, has a great expanse of forests and a more regular sequence of vegetation zones. The soils are of podzol type; however their quality is determined mainly by their texture. The vegetation form which succeeds the forests is not true tundra but rather an association of mosses, lichens, and shrubs which resembles Alpine vegetation and is colloquially described in Swedish as *fjällhed* (mountain heath).

In an area characterized by such diversity and so many nuances, standards testify to a wide and ancient unity of culture and nowadays of civilized life. Northern Europe (the Faroe Islands and Iceland excepted) was settled by immigrants from the south and east following the retreat of the Finland icesheets. But it was not until the expansion of the Scandinavian peoples in the Viking age (A.D. 800–1000) that the first real contribution was made to the unity and expansion of Norden culture.

Linguistic affinities are strong, the more so when it is noted that the spoken languages of Iceland and the Faroes correspond to archaic forms of the Norden languages. Finnish and Same (Lapp) belong, however, to completely different language families. The peoples of Northern Europe have never lived in total isolation and have long-standing and indirect contacts with Mediterranean civilization, for example, links with Western and Central Europe in the religious field (as in the conversion to Christianity and later the Reformation) and in the economic field (e.g., the Hanseatic League). Amongst the countries of Northern Europe, however, the bounds of historical solidarity that grew up later were far stronger, and it is precisely these special historical factors which prevent the inclusion in Norden of the Kola peninsula, northern Russia, and Scotland.

This cultural unity has been demonstrated more vigorously than ever during the last hundred years. It was facilitated by the relatively early disappearance or, indeed, absence of a feudal tradition and has found expression in a general will to achieve social equality, a concern for the early introduction of compulsory education, and an early development of folk high schools. Today the laws of the different Norden countries are in some cases identical word for word. The Norden countries have the system of social security and old age pensions for everybody. All over the region, co-operative movements play a major role. Not only cultural but also economic links are close, being facilitated by maritime transport. With the exception of Iceland, the Norden countries provide a common labour market. And a striking contrast is presented between their relative backwardness compared with Western and Central Europe in the nineteenth century and their spectacular progress in this century. Certainly Iceland and Sweden at least enjoyed peace and suffered no military occupation over a long period. The Norden countries rank today among the most advanced in Europe in respect both of standard of living and of life expectancy. But although their community of interest is strong and their relations with each other close, the Norden countries do not seek political unity through federation.

The end of the nineteenth century marks a turning point for the economic development of Norden. At that time certain products of Northern Europe became indispensable to the economies of Western and Central Europe. This was notably the case with pulp wood to meet the growing consumption of paper by daily newspapers. This was the case, too, with iron much earlier, although it was not until 1860 that it became technically possible to use to the full the ores of northern Sweden, and not until the end of the nineteenth and the beginning of the twentieth century that the workings in the extreme north were joined to the ports. (The railway from the iron-ore deposits in Kiruna to Luleå was opened in 1895 and that to Narvik in 1902.)

Norden lacks coal except for the deposit at Svalbard, the value of which is reduced by transport costs. The first modern industries depended in large measure on imported coal and remained located at the ports. Industrialization began first in Denmark. In the other Northern countries the technique of hydro-electric production has permitted the exploitation of rich hydraulic resources. Since the beginning of the twentieth century Norway has had the highest consumption of electricity per head in the world, followed by Canada, Sweden, and the United States. Even Finland, although less favoured because the levels of its lakes tend to be uniform, achieves a figure equal to that of France. Electricity has made possible the rapid development of electro-chemical and electro-metallurgical, as well as consumer, industries. Industrial workers are two to five times as numerous as agricultural workers—and a small agricultural labour force is a characteristic of highly developed countries. Industrial growth applies to all the Norden countries, and workers employed in industry are everywhere more numerous than those engaged in agriculture. In spite of the unfavourable natural conditions, cultivation and pastoral farming, using scientific methods, reaches levels which are among the highest in the world.

The countries of Northern Europe continue to draw from the sea an appreciable part of their resources. In fishing, Norway stands at the head of European countries (USSR excepted), followed by the United Kingdom, Iceland, Denmark (with the Faroes), Spain, and Sweden. Trade with the rest of the world is of the greatest importance to the economies of all the Norden countries. Even Iceland, with its population of 189,000, possesses seven packet-boats and twenty-three cargo ships (it is true, of low or medium tonnage). Numerous links exist with the United States, but the countries of Northern Europe trade also with the Soviet Union and would probably be the first to benefit from the expansion of the Soviet market.

This rapid development of industry and commerce is reflected in the high level of urban civilization and reflects a concern to develop resources rationally in the interests of the greatest number.

Norden is sparsely populated, the more so since it has provided numerous emigrants. The bulk of the population today is concentrated in relatively small areas as a result of strong industrialization. With a population of 20 millions, Norden accounts for only 3·5 per cent of that of Europe, although it occupies 16% of its area (Turkey included).

Delimitation of Northern Europe and Recommendations

The limits of Northern Europe or Norden are mainly maritime, although landwards it makes contact with Central Europe in southern Jutland and with Eastern Europe westwards of the Kola peninsula and beyond the eastern edge of the Finnish Lake Plateau. It comprises the following countries: Sweden, Norway, Denmark, Finland, the Faroe Islands (which are part of the Danish kingdom), and Iceland. Although Greenland is administratively a county of Denmark, it does not seem necessary to include this country, physically more American than European, in Norden. Svalbard (the Spitzbergen archipelago) can be treated either with Norway, and thus as part of Norden, or with other Arctic regions, according to the teaching programme. The terms 'Scandinavians' and 'Scandinavian countries' apply only to the central part of Northern Europe—namely, Norway, Sweden, and Denmark. However, the term 'Scandinavian peoples' applies to all the inhabitants of Norden.

EASTERN EUROPE

Eastern Europe is the region where Europe is broadest and, with increasing distance from the ocean, loses its peninsular character. It is bordered to the south and north by enclosed or semi-enclosed seas, —respectively by the Azov, Black, and Caspian, and the Baltic, White, and Barents Seas. While its historical limits to the west have changed continually, its physical limits there are clear. One can conceive of Eastern Europe as extending to adjoin Central Europe in the regions of the Vistula and San and as ending also in the south-west along the arc of the Carpathians. In the light of decisions already made at conferences devoted to other major regions of Europe, Eastern Europe, as defined by its neighbours, is the European part of the USSR as far eastwards as the Urals and the river Emba. However, this conventional eastern limit of Europe has no geographical reality, and, on certain grounds, Europe can be conceived to include parts of Northern Asia. In any case, the Soviet Union should not be divided into two parts for the purposes of geographical study.

First among the natural features which contribute to the individuality of Eastern Europe are its great area and extent. Eastern Europe alone occupies more than half of the territory of Europe, its north to south extent being some 2800 km. Together with the idea of immensity, its lack of articulation should be considered. There are places in Eastern Europe more than 1000 km. from the sea; subtle contrasts of sea and shore, plains and mountains, are little known here. Eastern Europe has only limited contacts, mainly through almost land-locked seas, with the Mediterranean and the North Sea lands, two cradles of European civilization.

The relief is dissected, yet characteristically monotonous, being made up essentially of low plateaux, cut by wide valleys asymmetrical in the south. European USSR is underlain at greater or lesser depth by the Pre-Cambrian Russian Platform and is rich in coal, associated with the Hercynian structure of the Donets Heights. The mountain chain of the Urals, also of Hercynian age, is favoured with a tremendous range of mineral wealth. Lands of youthful structure and high relief are found only in the Carpathians and the Crimea (as well as in the Asian part of the USSR in the Caucasus and in the lofty mountain chains bordering Central Asia). The Quaternary glaciations have strongly influenced the landscape throughout the whole of northern Russia, and to the south of the former limits of the ice-sheets extends a broad belt of loess.

Continentality is the key to the climates of European USSR. Of course, even Berlin is considerably affected by harsh winters, but eastwards of Berlin they become increasingly colder—and longer. Eastern Europe is a country with frozen rivers and with snow lying for a long time; during the period of thaw it suffers the *rasputitza*[1]. Some of the ports of the Baltic, all those of the White Sea, and even those of the Sea of Azov and the north Caspian freeze over in

---

[1] The "absence of ways". In contrast, when snow covers the ground, sledge routes can be found everywhere and mobility is ensured.

winter, although nowadays the use of ice-breakers may reduce the closed period. In contrast, Murmansk, on the north of the Kola peninsula, is open all the year.

This continental climate is not without regional variety. The following types have been distinguished and mapped (Alisov, 1956): Sub-Arctic in the extreme north, then moving southwards the Arcto-Atlantic, Atlantic-continental forest type, the Atlantic-continental steppe type, and the Continental-desert type in the area north of the Caspian Sea. Only in the southern Crimea does the Mediterranean type of climate intrude. As a result, there is a characteristic zonality of soils and vegetation distinguishing Eastern Europe from the rest of Europe. Two types of steppe, which are now under the plough, are found as one moves from south to north—grass steppe and wooded steppe. North of this extend in turn belts of deciduous forest, mixed forest, taiga (with its enormous reserves of wood), and tundra. We might add that similar vegetation zones stretch across great areas of Siberia in Soviet Asia; but to the south, in Soviet Middle Asia, as in the lower Volga basin, the USSR has to tackle the problems presented by arid zones including deserts.

The soils of European USSR are podzols, brown podzolic soils, black-earth soils (*chernozem*), chestnut-brown soils, and semi-desert soils in the extreme south-east of the steppe. Despite some soil erosion, the *chernozem* is renowned for its very great fertility, while the podzolized *chernozem* of the wooded steppe also gives high yields.

Finally, it is important to notice the part played by rivers which diverge to flow in all directions from the Valdai Hills. Despite their seasonal fluctuations in discharge, the Dnieper, Don, and Volga (3700 km.), especially the last-named, are valuable waterways. They have been used since prehistoric times, the more useful since portages were easy. Modern barrages, artificial lakes, and canals are renewing their importance.

In order to characterize Eastern Europe, it is necessary, despite the striking changes effected there since 1917, to take account of certain historical processes which were operative within this vast area of forests and steppe. Coming from the west and penetrating by way of the rivers, Slav-speaking intruders established themselves in the mixed forests and wooded steppes, avoiding the open steppe grasslands, and mingled within the forests with earlier mainly Finnic occupants.

Varangians (Northmen) settled among these people and reopened a trade route across Europe. From the Byzantine Empire to the south, also in the Middle Ages, these people derived their Cyrillic alphabet and their adherence to the Orthodox Christian Church. After the decline of Kievan Russia in the second half of the twelfth century, the principality of Muscovy was established astride the mixed forests and marshes of the upper Volga; with access along the rivers to the Baltic, Azov-Black, and Caspian Seas, and with its capital at Moscow, it became predominant. An inland State, at first of modest strength, Muscovy was the cradle of the Great Russian language and nation, poised ready to exploit its central position for purposes of colonization, trade, and territorial expansion. But Muscovy was long subject to strong pressures from its periphery, notably from the Mongol-Tartar hordes and later from the Lithuanians, Poles, Swedes, and Ottoman Turks. Even so, it grew strong enough to throw off the Mongol domination and steadily to colonize and to expand territorially in all directions, to the Arctic and Pacific shores and to those of the Baltic, Caspian, and Azov-Black Seas. Expansion to the last-named in the late eighteenth century involved the colonization and cultivation of steppe-lands which were to become a large source of surplus grain.

The Russia which thus succeeded politically in its prolonged efforts within a vast territorial frame, had come to acquire distinctive political, social, and economic characteristics which long persisted, serving to mark it off from the rest of Europe. Political power was concentrated in the hands of the Tsar who ruled over illiterate serfs with the aid of landowners, the Russian Church, an army, and a bureaucracy.

In the course of its expansion, Russia came to include peoples of different language, religion, and cultural tradition—Moslem communities, Lutheran Baltic peoples, and other Slav-speaking groups, notably the Belorussians and the Ukrainians. And although, in the time of Peter the Great, Russia was drawing on the superior scientific and technical knowledge of Western and Central Europe and had become the leading Slav nation and one of the great Powers of Europe, it was characterized by a static feudal society and a feudal agrarian economy, and by the lack of any strong liberal, democratic, and mercantile tradition, such as was developing in the West. As it had been bypassed by the Renaissance and the Reformation, so also it was scarcely affected by the revolutionary changes wrought elsewhere by the French Revolution. It is not surprising, therefore, that the new possibilities opened up by the industrial, agricultural, and transport revolutions of the eighteenth century made little impact on Russia until the second half of the nineteenth century, and then largely as the result of capital investment and initiatives which came from the West. Even so, substantial industrial progress was effected during the last decades of Tsarist Russia: witness the building of the railway system, the growth of extractive industries, the establishment of modern metallurgical industries (in European Russia) and of textile industries in Central Russia, the exploitation of Baku oil, the large-scale cultivation of cotton by irrigation in middle Asia, and the provision of large surpluses of timber and agricultural produce (grain and fibres) for export to Western Europe. Indeed, the economy of Tsarist Russia remained essentially based on agriculture (about 56 % by value) and the population was predominantly rural (80%). Further, almost the whole of its economic production (96%) was derived from its European territory west of, and including, the Urals.

In 1917 Russia produced its own revolution. Without doubt the USSR, as the successor to the Russian Empire, set itself to develop with great vigour and at fast pace the resources of Eastern Europe and Asiatic USSR. Until recently the emphasis has been put on the development of energy resources and on that of heavy industry, at the expense of consumer industry, as also of agriculture. With its large population (now over 225 millions) and its great area (8·6 million sq. miles, 22·4 million sq. km.), the Communist rulers of the USSR commanded immense resources, distributed very unequally over a country made up of sharply contrasting biogeographical zones—of tundra (27%), taiga and mixed forests (55%), steppes (10%), and deserts (8%). Continual effort to revalue the resources of the country has revealed enormous sources of energy, above all of coal and brown coal, but also of petroleum (especially in the Volga/Ural region), natural gas, and water power. Similarly, a wide range of minerals is available and many sources are exploited—resources of iron and non-ferrous metals, non-metallic minerals, and precious metal (gold, platinum, and silver), and diamonds.

The pace of industrialization has been rapid, notably on new sites east of the Volga, and the scale and complexity of Soviet heavy industries now rival those of the United States. Labour has been moved from the land to the industrial centres and the mines. Educational policy has eliminated illiteracy and produces an ever-growing supply of managerial and skilled labour. A policy of long-term planning has been consistently applied and emphasis has been put on the development of resources formerly neglected in the vast lands beyond the Volga as also in the European north and in south Caucasus.

The immense size of the USSR's territories, which for so long imposed great difficulties on imperial Russia, has proved an asset in this age of air navigation, mechanization, automation, and, in general, unprecedented scientific, technological, and economic possibilities. The taking over of all the resources by the State has meant that centralized plans can be systematically applied, so that a generation of Soviet citizens has been sacrificed to the future, restricting their own consumption (of housing, food, clothes, automobiles, etc.) in the interests of the growth of industry and those of State security. In the course of this industrialization, which has harnessed and directed the great energy of the Soviet peoples, old towns have expanded everywhere and new ones have been built, and great regions, formerly almost empty, are being steadily and sporadically colonized and developed. Soviet industrialization, as compared with that of Western, Central, and Northern Europe, came late, and has still a long way to go. It should be noted also that, despite all the many large-scale regional changes in the economy, it is Eastern Europe—*i.e.*, the territory west of, and including the Urals—which still dominates in respect of population number and production. In effect, what the USSR has achieved has been to extend Western civilization in its material cast throughout its vast Eurasian territory.

In respect of agriculture, the Soviet Union stands very high among the principal producers of grain, textile fibres, oilseeds, and beet sugar; so also in respect of timber and wood products. But the agricultural branch of the economy, despite socialization and mechanization, continually fails to achieve its production targets. Socialization meant the systematic creation of collective farms and the setting up of specialized State farms, but small private plots are held by peasants and contribute very substantially to supplies of milk, butter, eggs, vegetables, and fruit. Mechanization, so well suited to wide lowland areas, was applied to cultivation in order to reduce the rural labour force for the benefit of the industrial sector. As a result, Soviet farming consists mainly of the extensive kind of cultivation. In this respect the yields per hectare are low and much more manpower is employed than in North America. So far the USSR has sought to increase agricultural production by bringing into use more and more climatically marginal land, although some progress has been made by extending the irrigated area, and by improved agro-technical methods, and by an increasing use of chemical fertilizers. In fact, despite the variety of lands and climates, only 10 % of the USSR's territory is cultivated; the USSR commands at present only about half of the arable acreage per head available to the United States, and 70 % of this arable land (located in the steppe belts) has a rainfall both inadequate (less than 500 mm. a year) and, moreover, unreliable. But physical limitations apart, the relative failure of Soviet agriculture is due in part to policy decisions, notably the under-capitalization of agriculture, and to psychological considerations—the ideological difficulty of changing socialized forms of organization which fall far short of high efficiency. Another relevant factor is that the population increases steadily (by about 3·5 million a year) and that Soviet citizens (peasants as well as townsmen) enjoy a higher standard of living than ever before.

In short, Soviet (Marxist) socialist ideas and forms of social, economic, and political organization, which originated in Western and Central Europe, have found a wide field of application in Eastern Europe from which they have been carried to most of its Western neighbours in Central and Southern Europe; naturally, too, they have been introduced throughout the USSR's eastern territories, into Kazakhstan, Central Asia, and Siberia. In contrast with the rest of Europe, which is made up of national states, Eastern Europe forms part of the federally organized Union of Soviet Socialist Republics, so that seven well-developed national groups (Ukrainians, Byelorussians, Estonians, Lithuanians, etc.) form European member republics of the Union. These are organized into the following states: Lithuania, Latvia, Estonia, Byelorussia, Ukraine, Moldavia, and the RSFSR, the principle republic of the Union, which lies in both Europe and Asia. The greater Asiatic territories are organized on a similar national basis in eight member republics. As elsewhere in Europe, so in Eastern Europe and its borderlands, large political associations of independent states have been created for economic and defence purposes (COMECON and the Warsaw Pact Organization).

Delimitation of Eastern Europe and Recommendations

In physical geography the limits of Eastern Europe are found in the north in the borderlands between the USSR on the one hand, and Norway and Finland, on the other; to the east along the eastern foot of the Ural Mountains and along the Emba river; in the south along the Manych Depression and the eastern shore of the Azov Sea; in the west, where the USSR and Poland adjoin, in the lowland east of the Vistula-San rivers between the Carpathians and the Baltic, and also in the Carpathians and along the Prut river where the USSR adjoins Romania.

Eastern Europe consists politically of the territories of the Soviet Union which lie to the west of the eastern foot of the Urals. Thus Eastern Europe meets Northern Europe along the USSR/Norwegian and USSR/Finland boundaries; it adjoins Central Europe in the west, and approaches Southern Europe (along the USSR/Romania and the Turkey boundaries) in the south.

It is recommended to teachers and authors that the Soviet Union should be treated as a whole in geographical textbooks, since a division of it into a European and an Asiatic part has little or no meaning for geographers.

It is further recommended, following a decision made at the Bray Conference, that the geography of Romania in textbooks may be treated alongside that of Eastern Europe, or alongside that of either Central Europe or Southern Europe.

It is convenient also to include here the suggestions made on textbooks concerned with Eastern Europe which were accepted by the Conference as a whole. The wording is as follows:

(*a*) The terms 'Russia' and 'USSR' (Soviet Union) must be clearly distinguished. Up to 1917 'Russia' was the name given to the Russian Empire. Apart from the Russian Soviet Federal Socialist Republic (RSFSR), the biggest Union Republic of USSR, 'Russia' as a state no longer exists. The term 'USSR' or 'Soviet Union' is the only term covering the Federation of Soviet Republics in Europe and Asia.

(*b*) The extent to which Eastern Europe appears in textbooks varies greatly. Even though the uniformity of Eastern Europe compared to the geographical and political diversity of the rest of Europe might justify a shorter description, it should still be remembered that the size of Eastern Europe is roughly equivalent to the whole of the rest of Europe. The varying treatment of the larger European regions should, of course, depend on the relations of the country where the textbooks are published with the larger regions described. The space devoted to Eastern Europe and to the USSR should not neglect the significance of this area for the whole of Europe and the world.

(*c*) Since the inter-state organizations of the non-Communist States in Europe are described in the textbooks, it would likewise seem appropriate to pay attention to the links between the European Communist states themselves.

EUROPE'S UNDERLYING UNITY

It has been shown above that each of the five major parts of Europe has certain common environmental characteristics, both physical and social. On the one hand, each has its own specific location and, in a broad sense, its own climate; on the other, each reveals many common features of economic, social, and political life. This is not to say, however, that there are not marked diversities, within each major region, in respect of both physical and human geography. Even so, these major parts of the continent are properly to be regarded as geographical realities, the understanding of which contributes measurably to an understanding of Europe as a whole. But our characterization of these major parts should not obscure the fact that each has much in common with all the others. In other words, as was noted above, Europe possesses a certain degree of unity which underlies its very evident, yet perhaps overemphasized, diversities. And this unity resides not merely in the obvious physical fact that the continent is a nearly continuous area of land and bordering seas, but also in the community of its civilization.

From London to Moscow, from Stockholm to Athens, despite the contrasting landscapes which lie between and despite the many different tongues and the many nations, so often in the past opposed in war, a European never feels himself uprooted and never feels that he has moved outside a common homeland larger than his own. Doubtless Westminster Abbey, the City Hall of Stockholm, Notre-Dame in Paris, the Coliseum and St Peter's at Rome, and the Kremlin all characterize the very distinctive cities of well-established countries. Nevertheless these monuments appear to the European to be part of a common heritage, familiar to him because all were nourished by the same roots.

Realization of this fact is not new; it has developed little by little during the last 2500 years. Already the philosophers of ancient Greece distinguished Europe from Asia and from Libya (Africa). Their concept of Europe however, was admittedly vague, as was also their knowledge of its remoter parts. The Romans gave more reality to this concept as they opened up to their civilization, by conquest, regions towards and even beyond the Rhine and Danube. They were not slow to distinguish an inner Graeco-Roman continent which contrasted with that of the barbarians beyond their imperial limits. However, the intrusion of these peoples into the imperial territories during the period of the 'barbarian invasions' or

Völkerwanderung and their ultimate settlement and mingling with the pre-existing population infused new vigour. Thus, although the Empire in the West crumbled before their onslaughts, it regained, as did also the Empire in the East, cultural vitality. Indeed, Christian Europe in medieval times became culturally and politically strong enough to ward off domination by Asia, despite sundry temporary advances of the armies of the Mongol-Tartars and of the Arabs and Moors, and to lay the foundations for later cultural progress.

Europe, the smallest of the continents except Australasia, is also the one most fragmented, as a result of the changes brought by its long history, geological and human. That Europe has come to reconcile so many elements of diversity and yet to attain coherence is very much the product of human history. Indeed it is not difficult for the geographer to demonstrate that nature offered to Europeans regionally diverse and unequal opportunities within a favourable whole, and that they exploited these with conspicuous success.

Broadening eastwards, where it merges into Asia, Europe projects its southern peninsulas towards Africa and its western peninsulas and islands towards the Americas; moreover, it lies centrally within the northern or land hemisphere where the trade routes of the world converge. If civilization derives largely from the contacts of peoples and the diffusion of ideas and techniques, then by providing a meeting-place and a mixing-place for immigrant peoples, Europe was well placed to become the hearth of a new civilization. It was well placed, too, in modern times to make cultural contacts far afield and to diffuse its civilization—and emigrants—to many parts of the world.

Relief and climate acting together mark out large units and a swarm of differing regional entities. From north to south succeed in turn the Fennoscandian shield and East European (Sarmatian) platform, the extensive lowlands of the east and north, the Hercynian massifs with their deep sedimentary basins, and the various Alpine ranges from the Pyrenees to the Balkan and Anatolian ranges, enclosing within their arcs the cores of old massifs and lowlands or plateaux of some scale.

Europe lies in the belt of temperate climates which extend between lat. 35° and 60°N., and profits more than any other continent from the advantages of such climates, notwithstanding their marked regional variety. This is because the relief of Europe, disposed in parallel zones from west to east, opens it to the Atlantic, and because of the configuration of its coasts which allows the

D

Atlantic and the Mediterranean to penetrate deeply, thus giving even the interior of the continent some benefit from those maritime influences which characterize the western seaboard of continents in these latitudes. Thus in Europe, even at or near 60°N., in contrast to both Asia and North America, stand a number of great cities— Bergen, Oslo, Stockholm, Helsinki, and Leningrad. Certainly, for reasons of location and geological structure, Europe is climatically well endowed: but her destiny would have been very different if lofty mountain ranges, such as those on the Pacific side of North America, had confronted the Atlantic.

The climates of Europe then are favourable to human settlement and economy, yet reveal considerable regional and local diversity in response in no small degree to the remarkable diversities in the relief of the land. Remarkable diversities are evident no less in the human geography of the continent, notably in its patterns of languages, nations, and states. In the course of history the peoples of Europe, each settling down within its specific homeland, developed their own tongues. Within the Indo-European family of languages, for example, these are now such major groups as the Romance, Germanic, and Slavic, each including many distinct languages. Examples lying outside this family are those of the Finno-Ugrian and Turkic groups. It was primarily these many communities, as they developed their differing languages, which grew into nations attached to specific habitats, although in some cases other considerations than a common language were the main determinants of nation-making. For many Europeans actual consciousness of nationality, which produced the sentiment and creed of nationalism, came late—after the French Revolution of 1789—largely because claims to distinctiveness of culture and to political self-expression were long held in check by multi-national imperial states. However, in the present century nothing is more evident in Europe than the distinctness of its many nations, most of which have aspired to (and achieved) independent statehood, although others are organized together in federal states (*e.g.*, the USSR and Yugoslavia). At a time when the great empires existed (*e.g.*, in 1914) Europe accounted for 26 independent states (including four micro-states); in 1966, there were no fewer than 34 independent states and only two dependent ones—Andorra and Gibraltar.

Diversities are certainly fruitful for civilization so long as emulation does not lead to rivalry and degenerate into conflict. We recall that the history of Europe was often a sequence of unending wars. Let us recognize all the more that, despite so much wasted energy, the unremitting work of Europeans has totally modified the vegetation cover over a great part of the continent and has everywhere created great cities as a memorial to this endeavour. The European landscape demonstrates the power of human labour and creativity at its very best.

This creativity reminds us that Europe, despite the diversity of its languages, nations, and states, appears, especially when viewed from outside, a unit in one peculiarly important respect—that it has long been, and remains, a homeland of high civilization. This was originally derivative in that it received ideas and stimuli from neighbouring peoples in the Near East, to whom it owed its first civilized ways of life and the Christian religion. Yet, within itself, Europe has never failed to generate its own creativeness, alike in the field of intellectual, artistic, and practical endeavour. Within its own confines it has drawn from ancient Greece and Rome, from immigrant Jews and Moslems, from Byzantium and Renaissance Italy, from Portuguese, Spanish, and other discoverers, from German, French, and Swiss leaders in the Reformation. To the enrichment of life in its manifold aspects the peoples of Europe made continual contribution—to art and letters, to philosophy and law, to political ideas and organization, to science and technology, to the production of wealth, and to commerce. So resourceful and successful were they that their continent came to acquire a predominant status in the world, to which it diverted some of its energies by imperialism, colonization, trade, and capital investment. Moreover, in recent centuries Europe gave birth to a veritable revolution in industry, agriculture, and transport which provided the means greatly to increase the material welfare of mankind and, by reducing effective distance, opened up the prospect of a new unity of the world.

In its spiritual as distinct from its material manifestations European civilization appears to express a confidence in reason—in the conviction that human intelligence is able to understand and to control nature thanks to science and technology—in the proud affirmation that "man is the measure of all things". But it should not be forgotten that Europe is, for much the greater part, a Christian world. Thus the originality of Europe might well reside in the fact that, throughout its history, it accepted the co-existence of reason and faith; that, while it accepted the difficulties of this contradiction, it compelled itself to harmonize them in a higher synthesis.

If European civilization often appears challenging and intolerantly assertive, it is because it never yielded to those aggressive forces which are born and thrive in every human society; in particular, it never yielded to the perpetual attack on human liberty by all forms of subjection, political, economic, and social. Beyond doubt Europe has been oppressed and disgraced by some of the worst tyrannies, but it has witnessed also, throughout the whole of its history, the most glorious struggles for liberty.

The twentieth century, with its continual political and social crises and its more costly and bloody wars, might seem to mark the decline of Europe and to relegate it brusquely to a mere appendage of Asia. But its large (and highly skilled) population—nearly one-fifth of mankind—continues to give it great vitality. Even the division into two camps (East and West) becomes a source of competition and of progress and, paradoxically, for this continent of paradoxes, might prove conducive to its ultimate unity. Thanks to its factories, ships, and aircraft, its science and technology, its literature and other arts, and its political and social ferment, Europe confidently makes its way, facing new challenges at every turn, yet aspiring towards a still stronger unity born of the increasingly close collaboration of its peoples in thought and in action.

National Contributions

AUSTRIA

The Republic of Austria was formed after the First World War out of the German-speaking countries of the former Danubian monarchy. With its 84,000 sq. km. and its 7 million inhabitants, it surpasses Switzerland in both area and population. Austria extends over a length of 560 km. between *Lake Constance* in the west and the *Neusiedler Lake* in the east. The eastern Alps take up two-thirds of its area. Its hills and fertile basins are situated mainly in the north and east of the country. Austria is thus both an *Alpine* and *Danubian* country. Its most densely populated and economically important areas border on the Danube on whose banks, at the country's eastern extremity, lies *Vienna*, the capital.

The Austrian mountains offer a variety of landscapes. In the centre there are the *Central Alps* composed of crystalline rocks such as gneiss, granite, and mica-schist. In the west the mountains are high and sheer and covered with many glaciers; the highest ranges are the *Otztaler Alps* and the *Hohe Tauern*. Towards the east the Alps become lower and their forms softer. To the north and south of the Central Alps the *limestone* Alps raise their steep crests, picturesque rock peaks, or isolated plateaux above sheer cliffs. Circulation within the Alps is made easier by the big, longitudinal *Inn*, *Salzach*, and *Enns* valleys in the north and the *Mur* and *Drau* valleys in the south, all interlinked by numerous passes. The Alps provide the economy with a wealth of hydraulic power, broad summer pastures (alpine pastures), and, above all, extensive pine forests. Austria is one of the most *wooded* countries of Europe; roughly half the area of Styria is covered by forest. Austria owes its reputation as a *tourist* country to the natural beauty of the Alps.

Austria is a *Federal State* composed of provinces or federal *Länder*, Vienna being both the federal capital and a federal *Land*. Each of the Austrian *Länder* has an autonomous life. In the west the *Vorarlberg*, the *Tirol*, and the provinces of *Salzburg* remind one very much of Switzerland. The local peasantry utilize the meadows and pastures for extensive stock breeding. Summer and winter many foreigners visit the spas and sports centres of these provinces, notably *Badgastein*, *Kitzbühel*, and the *Arlberg* region. Almost all of Austria's famous skiers come from this part of the country. The rivers are harnessed more and more for the production of energy.

The big power stations astride the *Ill* in the Vorarlberg send current as far as the Ruhr. The broader valleys, such as the Rhine and Inn valleys, have also attracted many factories; the Vorarlberg textiles have a good reputation. *Innsbruck*, the capital of the Tirol, is also a university and mountaineering centre. It is here that the major lines of communication converge towards Italy via the *Brenner*. *Salzburg* is situated at the foot of the Alps where the very popular Salzach valley emerges from the mountains. Its picturesqueness is well known and music lovers from all over the world attend its festivals devoted to Mozart, the town's most famous son.

The southern province of *Carinthia*, a country of mountains and lakes, is a popular summer resort. Austria's highest mountain, the *Grossglockner*, dominates the frontier between Carinthia and the Tirol. An audaciously conceived highway crosses the mountain at this point. *Klagenfurt*, the capital of the province, lies in the midst of a fertile basin. With its wooded mountains, eastern Carinthia resembles neighbouring *Styria*, called on account of its wealth of forests the 'green province' (*grüne Mark*). In Carinthia and Styria there are many sawmills, and wood, cellulose, cardboard, and paper mills. In both provinces there are magnesium mines, the magnesium being used in the production of non-inflammable materials; the lignite deposits provide fuel and energy for the steam-power plants which supplement the production of the hydraulic plants. The province of Styria is also rich in iron ore: the *Erzberg* north of Leoben contains one of Europe's main iron deposits; the mine is worked on the surface. A part of the iron ore is treated and transformed into rails at *Leoben-Donawitz*. In the *Mur* and *Mürz* valleys various steel-processing industries process a series of plants; a high-grade electric-steel is produced at *Kapfenberg*. *Graz*, the capital of Styria, also has big factories and is, in addition, an important university town. To the south and east of Graz there is a broad area of fertile hills where even the vine is cultivated. The *Burgenland*, a belt of land along the Hungarian frontier, is an essentially flat and fertile region where the vine, fruit trees, vegetables, and maize flourish during long and hot summers.

However, over half the Austrian population lives in the northern provinces, particularly in the low areas and basins bordering on the Danube. The north of *Upper Austria* and of *Lower Austria* consists of plateaux which are still partially wooded. To the south these two provinces stretch deep into the limestone Alps which are abundantly covered in forest and contain salt in the *Salzkammergut* in Upper

Austria. In the centre the undulating *fore-Alps* stretch from west to east: they comprise fertile agricultural land, big towns, the principal industrial plants, and the main lines of communication. The frontier town of *Braunau* has a big aluminium factory which draws its electrical energy from the power plants on the Inn and Danube. Near the confines of the Alps wood is turned into cardboard, paper cellulose, and rayon. The towns of *Linz* and *Steyr* are industrial centres. In Linz, the capital of Upper Austria, the *Vereinigte österreichische Eisen- und Stahlwerke* (VOEST) transform national and imported iron ore into crude steel and sheet metal; nearby, a nitrogen factory produces chemical fertilizers. The old steel town of Steyr produces motor-cars, tractors, and ball bearings.

The lowlands of Lower Austria are the country's most fertile area. Here wheat, sugar beet, and vines are grown extensively. In the *Weinviertel* (wine-growing area), in the province's north-eastern angle, there are important petroleum and gas reserves. *Vienna*, situated where the Danube flows into the Danube basin, is one of Europe's largest towns. Magnificent buildings dating back to the imperial era border on the Ring, which, on the site of the old fortification, encircles the old town. Its university and colleges make it an important cultural centre. In the west, along the edge of the Wienerwald, lies the villa quarter, while the industrial suburbs are situated to the south and east. Here every conceivable kind of finished product is manufactured, but the clothing and leather industries have a particularly good reputation.

Compared with Switzerland, Austria has better natural resources, but it has had to bear the vicissitudes of history for much longer. Its cultivated surface is larger than that of Switzerland, and in the east the summers are sufficiently hot to permit the most fragile plants and the vine to flourish. The use of chemical fertilizers and machines has caused an appreciable rise in yield. As the *livestock* is considerable and milk production has been improved, Austria is today able to meet some 85 % of its needs in foodstuffs out of its own production. There are, in addition, large exports of cattle. The *forest* represents great wealth. The converted timber is exported, above all to Italy, and paper and cellulose also form an important export.

In addition, *industry* can draw on considerable natural resources: lignite, petroleum, iron ore, magnesite, salt, graphite, and hydro-electric power abound and are exploited more and more. There are successive dams on the waterways, including the Danube. The *Aschach* power station on the Danube, the country's biggest, furnishes almost a tenth of the over-all energy production, which attains some 18 thousand million kWh. On the other hand, the factories' needs in coal and coke have to be met by imports. Some 4 million tons of iron ore are extracted annually; the treatment centres are at Linz and Leoben-Donawitz, while processing also takes place at Steyr and in the towns watered by the Mur and Mürz. Machines, vehicles, and apparatus are manufactured primarily in Vienna and Graz. The *paper and cellulose industry* has established itself mainly along the rivers which flow at the foot of the Alps, and the *textile industry* in the Vorarlberg and the Vienna basin. Other consumer goods are manufactured in all medium-sized towns. Over half of Austria's exports are today made up of machines, transport equipment, and other finished products; a quarter of semi-finished products (converted timber, sheet metal, etc.); and only the remaining quarter of raw materials such as lumber, iron ore, and foodstuffs. Austria's main trading partners today are its neighbours—Germany and Italy.

Trade flows are thus mainly with the west and the south. The chief axes are the western railway-line (Vienna–Linz–Salzburg–Innsbruck–Arlberg Tunnel, and, beyond, Switzerland); the highway running parallel to this railway-line; and the Vienna–Linz–Salzburg motorway. Traffic between Vienna and the south-west goes through the Semmering pass and then through Graz to Yugoslavia, or through Klagenfurt to Italy. The main transverse line of communication links southern Germany with Italy through the Brenner. In the summer there is heavy traffic on the routes which lead from Salzburg across the Alps, particularly on the Tauern railway and the Grossglockner highway. Navigation on the Danube is increasing, although trade with the Danubian countries is relatively unimportant. The main overseas port for Austria is Trieste in Italy, but the external trade also passes through the German North Sea ports. *Tourism* is of primary importance to Austria. As imports always exceed exports, the profits derived from tourism serve to restore the balance. Most of the foreign tourists come from neighbouring Germany and visit the western provinces. During the last twenty years many hotels have been built and others enlarged in this area. The number of rooms made available in private houses has followed the steeply rising curve of the number of visitors.

During the last fifty years Austria has had to travel a hard road: formerly the centre of a big empire, it has become a small country which has had to reorganize its economy and trade relations entirely.

Austria has, moreover, been sorely tried by fate: annexed by Germany in 1938, it suffered human losses, the destruction of the Second World War, and, after the war, occupation by foreign troops. With the aid of ERP (European Recovery Programme), it has succeeded not only in rebuilding its ruins but in raising its economic output considerably. Today Austria is, in the heart of Europe, an industrial country with a sound economy which trades with many countries.

DR H. LECHLEITNER
Department of Geography
Vienna School of Economics and Business Administration

BELGIUM

I. THE BELGIAN COUNTRYSIDE AND AGRICULTURE

A small country with an area of only 30,500 sq. km. but a population of 9·3 million, Belgium has a certain variety of landscapes, forming as it does part of the European plain and possessing a Hercynian mountain range, the Ardennes.

(a) The Coast

Along the Belgian coast there is a chain of seaside towns extending on both sides of Ostend (Oostende); the towns are separated by dunes behind which lie the Polders (dried-up coastal marshes) with their lush cultivation and meadows intersected by drainage canals. Belgium is a country of large farms and very small villages; there is only one large town on the southern boundary, Bruges (Brugge), in which there are beautiful medieval monuments and an industrial suburb.

(b) The Northern Plain

In the west Flanders (Vlannderen) is entirely cultivated thanks to close on a thousand years of labour (the soil consisting of a mixture of surface sand and underlying clay, with the addition of farm manure); trees abound throughout a multitude of small fields, two-thirds of whose produce goes to feed cattle. The small farms are scattered between the large villages, a large part of whose populace works in factories or trades which are either isolated or concentrated in towns. The numerous and densely populated towns are situated on rivers (Scheldt) or streams (Lys), like Courtrai (Kortrijk), Ghent (Gent), Antwerp (Antwerpen), Malines (Mechelen).

In southern Flanders the soil is marshy and suitable for the growing of wheat and industrial plants (flax).

In the east the soil is made up of the coarse sands of Campine (Kempen), one-third of whose surface is still covered by moorland heaths and pine forests. An area with a high birthrate, Campine has long been a source of supply of manpower to other areas, but is now itself becoming industrialized.

(c) The Low Marsh Plateaux

Of an altitude of between 50 and 200 m., the low plateaux of central Belgium are intersected by broad valleys, with rising uplands towards the plain. The broad, open countryside between the large villages with their prosperous farms is devoted to the growing of cereals and sugar beet, the fattening of cattle, and the breeding of horses for the plough (despite competition from the tractor).

(d) The High Plateaux of the South

To the south of the Charleroi–Liège (Sambre and Meuse valley) industrial axis, the primary stratum of the plateaux, which are intersected by deep valleys, bears only a thin layer of soil and is covered by forest; here more space is occupied by meadows and fields of fodder plants than by wheat fields. According to the nature of the subsoil, the area may be divided into four distinct regions: Condroz, with its sandstone ridges separated by limestone depressions a region of quarries and large farms (*châteaux*); the wooded area of Herve, east of Liège, with its subsoil of clay, consisting only of pastures; the Ardennes, rising to between 300 and 600 m., densely wooded but with many green slopes, with a severe and humid climate, thinly populated (38 inhabitants per sq. km. against 300 in Flanders) and a popular tourist area; and Belgian Lorraine, with its cuesta uplands (secondary sandstone and limestone), fairly fertile in the south and more densely populated than the Ardennes. The townlets are merely small market towns (for example, Bastogne), tourist centres (Dinant), or administrative centres (Arlon). The sole industrial centre is Verviers, situated between the Ardennes and the Herve area.

Intensive and advanced (improvements, fertilizers, mechanization), Belgian agriculture nevertheless accounts for only 7% of the national income; taking up 56% of the land (half of which consists of meadows) and divided up into small plots (an average of 8·7 ha. per holding), it provides work for only 7% of the country's active population. It is nevertheless a mixed agriculture with a high yield. It is estimated that the agriculture meets four-fifths of the population's food requirements; a number of agricultural products are, moreover, exported (fruit, vegetables, eggs, pork).

II. INDUSTRIAL AREAS AND PROBLEMS

In Belgium 45% of the population work in industry which comprises a vast number of small- and medium-sized undertakings; industries with over 500 workers employ only 10% of the labour force. The most important industries are basic metallurgy and processing (30%), textiles (20%), and food (12%).

The country as a whole is intersected by two main axes:

(1) A north–south axis whose focal points are the port of Antwerp, where imported energy products and raw materials enter (36·5 million tons), and the capital, Brussels. A navigation canal, broad highways, and railway-lines run alongside this axis, serving a multitude of industries of all kinds: petrol refineries, coke and chemical products, non-ferrous metals, shipbuilding, textiles, etc.

The industries are spread out on either side of the axis: to the west the textile towns of Flanders including Ghent, with a belt of mixed industry bordering a canal leading to the sea; to the east, in the Campine, plants treating non-ferrous metals, a nuclear centre (Mol), glassworks, a coal basin producing rich coal, workshops.

(2) A west–east axis across the old coal basin of Wallonia, which is intersected by the Meuse, Sambre, and canals. Here there is a concentration of heavy industry (steel, non-ferrous metals, chemical products), metal structures, and glassworks, particularly around the two focal points, Charleroi and Liège.

Also within their orbit are the wool region of Verviers and, in the extreme south, the steel works of Athus, which are adjacent to French Lorraine and the Grand Duchy of Luxembourg.

An industrial country, Belgium sells half of its output abroad; indeed, exports of chemical products amount to 75%, of non-ferrous metals to 70%, and of glassware to 90%. Belgium's rate of industrial growth is, however, lower than that of the other countries of the European Economic Community—namely, 150 against an average of 190.

(a) Belgium's sole indigenous energy resources are its coal; it has to import all its petrol, natural gas, and all its raw materials. In view of the coal market conditions as against those of other energy sources and as a result of the country's integration in an economic community, Belgian coalmining output has in the last ten years fallen from 30 to 20 million tons; this decline is, however, due solely to the fact that Wallonia has had to close half of its mines as being uneconomical; parts of its basin, particularly in the west (Borinage and Central Hainaut), are therefore in the throes of a serious economic depression; they are, however, slowly being reconverted as a result of the development of new industries. On the other hand, the Campine coal basin is holding its own: it has seven modern coalmines producing 10 million tons.

(*b*) Heavy industry also has a drawback: traditionally, its production is concentrated on unfinished and semi-finished goods and therefore has to face greater competition on the markets. Gradual conversion is taking place with a view to the manufacture of more elaborate products involving more specialized manpower in the basic industry areas of Charleroi and Liège and, above all, as the result of the erection of new plant, along the Brussels–Antwerp axis in Flanders and Campine, where there are manpower reserves.

(*c*) Industrial enterprise is therefore more dynamic in north Belgium owing to the proximity of the sea and to a more densely concentrated network of inland waterways; there are basic industries in the area (coke, non-ferrous metals, chemical products) and the steel industry itself is undergoing development (modern complex to the north of Ghent).

III. THE UNIFIED STATE AND THE NATIONAL PROBLEM

Belgium is composed of two main communities with a separate language: the Flemish community in the north whose language is Flemish; the Walloon community in the south whose official language is French. The Brussels area in the centre is bilingual administratively, but French is the language more widely used (75%). Under recent laws the administrative boundaries have been made to coincide with the language frontier. Apart from the population of Brussels, there are 5 million Flemings, 3 million Walloons, and some 75,000 German-speaking inhabitants in the eastern areas.

(*a*) In this unified and centralized country the Flemings are in a clear majority; they have the advantage of a high average birthrate, extensive manpower resources, the proximity of the sea and the port of Antwerp (third port of Europe handling 55 million tons of merchandise), a coal basin which holds its own, and a sound infrastructure.

(*b*) The population of Wallonia, on the contrary, increases only very slowly (1000 more Walloons per year as against 41,000 Flemings). Wallonia has an ageing population, its coal-mines are disappearing, it is losing its steel industry monopoly, many of its industrial plants are obsolete, and its infrastructure is generally inadequate. Wallonia therefore feels that it suffers the fate of a minority. Its yearly income growth rate per inhabitant was only 1·9 from 1955 to 1963, as against 2·9 in Flanders and 3·1 in Brussels. It received only 18% of foreign investments as against 71% in northern Belgium.

Problems therefore exist in both the demographic and economic spheres, in regard to regional development and the very structure of the State. Yet in this small, highly populated, industrialized country, whose external trade represents 3·2% of world trade, the various economic areas remain interdependent. Seeking to maintain a sound balance between them, the State continues to study the improvements and reconversion measures needed and to take appropriate action.

J. TILMONT
Inspecteur Général
Brussels

CYPRUS

Introduction

Cyprus lies in the Eastern Mediterranean at the crossroads of three continents—Asia, Africa, and Europe. It has an area of 9250 sq. km. and is in size the third island in the Mediterranean. Its distance from Turkey to the north is 65 km., from Syria to the north-east, 100 km., from Egypt to the south, 400 km., and from Rhodes to the west, 430 km. The island's proximity to three continents has brought it into contact with the great Near Eastern cultures of the past, but at the same time has laid it open to conquest by the various Powers which in the course of history have dominated the Near East—Assyria, Egypt, Persia, Rome, the Crusaders, Venice, Turkey, and Britain.

Of all the cultures with which the island came into contact, the Greek culture brought in by the Mycenaean Greeks, who colonized the island towards the end of the second millennium B.C., was so deeply rooted that it held its own and did in fact prevail despite the adversities held in store for the Cypriot people.

I. PHYSICAL GEOGRAPHY

(a) Physical Features

Cyprus may be divided into three major physical regions—the Troodos Massif, in the south, the Pentadactylos Range to the north, and the Mesaoria Plain ranging in width from 15 to 20 km. between the two.

The core of the Troodos Massif consists of igneous rocks, both plutonic and volcanic. The extrusive rocks consist almost wholly of pillow-lavas, which were extruded beneath the sea. In these are found the rich deposits of iron and copper pyrites, which comprise by far the largest mineral exports of the island. The plutonic rocks contain deposits of asbestos and chromite.

The Troodos Massif is surrounded by sedimentary rocks such as clays, chalks, marls, and limestones, ranging in age from Upper Cretaceous to Pliocene. The long and narrow Pentadactylos Range consists mainly of limestones, chalk, and marls, ranging in age from Permian to Pliocene. It was formed during the Alpine Orogenetic movement.

E

Of all the rocks of Cyprus, the chalks and the marls are the most liable to erosion. Owing to rejuvenation the Troodos Massif has a 'young' appearance, with steep slopes and deep valleys.

The Mesaoria Plain consists mainly of Miocene and Pliocene sediments of great thickness. The Pliocene deposits include shelly-limestones, which have led to the formation of 'mesas', a characteristic feature of the lowlands.

Karstic phenomena are met with in the Pentadactylos Range. Subterranean deposits feed the big springs of Lapithos and Kythrea.

(b) Climate

The climate of Cyprus is typical of the Eastern Mediterranean, with rainfall limited to nine or even fewer months of the year. Temperature and rainfall vary according to locality and topography. Thus Nicosia, the capital in the central plain, has an average temperature of 10°C. in January and 29·4°C. in August, the hottest month of the year, an annual range of 19·4°C. On the other hand, Limassol, on the south coast, has an average temperature of 11·1°C. in January and 27·7°C. in August. Amiandos, a mining village on the Troodos Range (height 4450 ft), has an average January temperature of 3·6°C. and an average August temperature of 23·4°C.

The average annual rainfall at Nicosia is about 12 in. and falls for only some fifty days in the year. At Limassol it is about 16 in., and at Amiandos, on the Troodos Range, it is 38 in. and is spread over about eighty days. The Mesaoria Plain may have very hot days, the thermometer sometimes reaching 40·5°C., but there is a sharp drop at night, which makes evenings comfortable.

Vegetation follows the climatic pattern. There are coniferous forests on the mountains. The carob tree, whose bean is a valuable product, grows on the slopes and the plains along the coasts. The Mesaoria Plain, the granary of the island in the winter, is practically devoid of any natural vegetation and in the summer has the appearance of a semi-desert.

Irrigation naturally plays an important part in agriculture. Since the island's independence more dams for storing water have been built across the valleys of rivers coming down from the Troodos Mountains.

Parallel with water conservation, afforestation is being carried on in many areas. Forests cover 19% of the total area, and act as a check on soil erosion on the mountain slopes, where its effects could be catastrophic.

II. HUMAN GEOGRAPHY

(a) Agriculture

Cyprus is predominantly an agricultural country, since 40% of the economically active population are engaged in agriculture. The Central or Mesaoria Plain has been the island's granary; in places like the Famagusta region, however, and the Morphou region, where there are adequate supplies of underground water, farmers have turned to citrus-growing. Citrus fruits account for 17·7% of the exports. Other profitable export crops are potatoes (10·3% of the exports) and carrots.

The excessive use of underground water supplies has led to a drop in the level of the water-table. The construction of dams will help in the conservation of water.

Animal husbandry is carried on in the drier parts of the lowlands and in unforested mountain areas. The animals—sheep and goats—can live on the sparse winter grass; grazing, however, becomes difficult in the dry summer.

The carob and olive thrive particularly along the coasts. Olive oil is an indispensable part of the diet in the Mediterranean.

(b) Industry

Until recently industrial activity in the island was very limited and was concerned mainly with the production of wines and spirits, soft drinks, and cigarettes. Local demand has led to the production of commodities like ready-made clothes, furniture, and chemicals. Growing demand from abroad has led to the further growth of the wine and spirits industries and the canning of fruit and vegetables.

Despite the limitation to industrial growth, resulting from the lack of fuels and minerals, there has been recently a growing drop in the number of people living in rural areas and an increase in the urban population. The proportion was 23% in 1881, 25% in 1921, and 56% in 1960. This has led to the speedy growth of some of the cities like Nicosia, Limassol, and Famagusta, at the expense of the countryside.

People from the countryside do not only move to the towns but a number of them emigrate abroad, mainly to the United Kingdom. Since 1955, 68,454 Cypriots have left the island. This number includes people from the countryside as well as the towns.

(c) Tourism

Cyprus has vast possibilities for tourism. The island's mild
Mediterranean climate and its beautiful coastal and mountain
scenery, as well as its archaeological sites and historical monuments,
are a great attraction to tourists from the Near East and Europe.
The improvement in air and sea communications, and in the road
system within the island, and the construction of many new hotels
as well as the comparatively low cost of living will no doubt contribute to the growth of tourism. Visitors to Cyprus increased from
32,000 in 1955 to 70,000 in 1963 when the contribution to the national
income from tourists amounted to £4·5 million.

(d) Foreign Trade

Cyprus has to import many of the goods necessary for its economic development, particularly machinery and other manufactured
goods.

The exports are mainly agricultural products (citrus fruit,
potatoes, carobs, carrots, barley, raisins and sultanas, and alcoholic
beverages) and minerals (cupreous concentrates, iron pyrite, asbestos). The gap in the balance of payments is made up by income
from tourism, from remittances from abroad, and from income
derived from servicemen living in the British bases.

(e) Population

According to the latest census (1960), the island's population
stood at 577,615, of whom 448,857 are Greeks, 104,350 Turks, and
24,408 British, including those of the Base areas. The Turkish minority, along with the other minorities, has been an inseparable part
of the population. Turks and Greeks have lived side by side in the
towns and many of the villages for three centuries, and Turkish
villages lie scattered among the Greek villages.

(f) Administration

The island is divided for administrative purposes into six districts,
taking their names from their respective capitals. The town population ranges from 95,515 inhabitants in Nicosia, the capital, to
3498 in Kyrenia, the smallest town (Census of 1960).

F. S. MARATHEFTIS
Lecturer in Geography
Pedagogical Academy of Cyprus

DENMARK

The Kingdom of Denmark consists of the peninsula of Jutland and about 100 inhabited and 400 uninhabited islands. The total area (Greenland not included) is 43,000 sq. km., and the population in 1968 was 4·8 million, which gives a density of 112 per sq. km. In Western Europe only Luxembourg, Belgium, the Netherlands, and Switzerland are smaller in area than Denmark, and only Iceland, Luxembourg, the Republic of Ireland, Norway, and Finland have a smaller population.

The seas surrounding Denmark are shallow, and if their beds rose 100 m. Jutland would be joined to Great Britain and—via the islands of Funen and Zealand—to Sweden. Few industrialized countries are as dependent on access to the sea as Denmark, which both utilizes the rich fishing grounds of the North Sea and the Baltic and participates in the heavy traffic across and around those waters.

Geographical Location

The extreme north-westerly location of Denmark, as long as it lay on the outer edge of the known world, proved a disadvantage, and accordingly many cultural currents reached Denmark late. On the other hand, the remoteness has made it possible for Denmark to maintain her independence continuously for more than 1000 years. Recent development of the system of communications and the increasing importance of the Scandinavian countries both as producers and as trade-partners have changed the location to a more central one; international highways and important railroads cross Denmark, the harbour of Copenhagen is the most important in the Baltic, and the airport of Kastrup (Copenhagen) ranks fifth in Europe.

Landforms and Relief

The Danish landscapes originate almost completely from glacial and post-glacial times. Three (or four) times the Scandinavian glaciation affected Denmark, the last time leaving the south-western part of Jutland outside the glaciated area. Moraine landscapes, therefore, dominate, the hilly marginal moraine landscape and the moraine-flat being of equal importance. In south-west Jutland out-wash plains from the glacial rivers are found in the lower parts between the older moraine-hills of the second glaciation, which were not overridden. During the glaciation large parts of Denmark sunk locally more than 50 m. below today's level. Recent emergence has, particularly in the northern parts, added considerable areas of marine foreland to the shores and has thus created attractive recreation areas.

No point in Denmark exceeds 600 ft, and nowhere are the hills so steep that they cannot be used for agriculture. Most of the Danish soils are relatively fertile, the moraine-flats being of the highest quality, the outwash-plains of the lowest; but everywhere the intensive farming system makes cultivation completely dependent on a considerable use of imported fertilizers.

Climate

The climate of Denmark is dominated by the prevailing westerly winds and is of the temperate maritime type. The summers are moderately warm (July 15°C. in the west, 17°C. in the east), and the winters are comparatively mild (February 0°C.). The precipitation is normally sufficient for crops and forests, and irrigation is of little importance. A general complaint is that sunshine is too scarce and wind and rain too common.

Vegetation

Linked to the changes in climate since the glaciers left Denmark, the natural vegetation has altered from a sparse polar tundra vegetation to forests, coniferous trees being the first to arrive, but soon giving way to deciduous trees (oak, and, later, beech). With the introduction of agriculture and particularly husbandry 5000 years ago, the forests suffered badly, and today little of the original forest is left. Modern reafforestation has repaired some of the losses, and at the moment 11 % of Denmark is forested, but all forests are cultivated, and spruce is the dominant tree.

Population

The population of Denmark numbers 4·8 millions (1968), and the density is 112 (compared to 17 in Sweden and 12 in Norway). Birth and death rates are 18·0 % and 10·1 % respectively, and the annual increase is 7·9 %, or approximately 40,000.

National minorities are unimportant; only in the southern parts, near the German border, is found a small minority of German-speaking people (about 40,000). Emigration and immigration balance at about 30,000.

Denmark is highly urbanized; little more than 25% live under rural conditions; the same fraction of the population is found in Copenhagen, and the rest in urban settlements, none of which has more than 200,000 inhabitants. All the towns of more than 30,000 inhabitants are harbours, and among the inland towns only five (Herning, Silkeborg, Viborg, Slagelse, and Hillerød) exceed 20,000. The rural part of the population originally lived in villages, but the last century saw a movement from the villages to separate farms (*cf.* the English Enclosure Movement).

The Economy

Owing to the fact that Danish bacon, butter, and meat are well-known products in industrialized, food-importing countries, Denmark is normally considered predominantly an agricultural country. This is, however, not true today. Agriculture and forestry occupy only 13% of the gainfully occupied population, industry, etc., 35%, trade 12%, transport 7%, fisheries less than 1%, and administration and the professions 20%; and among exports, industrial goods exceed agricultural products.

The inhabitants of Denmark enjoy a comparatively high standard of living judged by traditional measuring-rods. In terms of gross domestic product per capita Denmark ranks ninth in the world, and in Europe only Switzerland, Sweden, and Luxembourg reach a higher level. This result has been achieved in spite of the fact that Denmark is poor in mineral resources. Great emphasis has, therefore, been laid upon specialization and upon high quality, though the Danish market has always handled all kinds of production, all-important products from both agriculture and industry competing in the foreign market, making Denmark to a great extent dependent on a smooth and liberal participation in foreign trade.

Agriculture

Sixty-three per cent of the total area is arable land and 7% under permanent grass; few countries—if any—utilize a corresponding proportion of their area. Danish farming is of an intensive, highly mechanized type (on 160,000 farms more than 170,000 tractors are used, combines gather in by far the bigger part of the grain-harvest, hand-milking is found only locally, etc.). This demands a high level of investment and makes high yields both necessary and possible (the yields per hectare for wheat and barley compete with those of the Netherlands).

Medium-sized farms dominate the agricultural landscape, but small-holdings still play an important role, whereas big estates occupy only a small percentage of the farmland. The Danish farmers have always tilled their farms individually, done the harvesting with the help of hired manpower, and looked after their own cattle. The well-known Danish co-operative movement has been concerned only with further processing of the agricultural products, and with distribution and trade (co-operative dairies, slaughter houses, egg-packing factories, etc., co-operatives for providing foodstuffs, fertilizers, and machinery).

Fodder-crops dominate Danish farming completely (less than 10% of the harvest is used directly for human food). Sixty per cent of the cropped area is in grains (barley 40%, oats 10%, wheat and rye 5% each); beets for fodder, oil-seeds, and sugar beets are also important. Normally Denmark must import grains, but has a surplus of sugar and oil-seeds.

Relative to population, no country in the world has so many pigs as Denmark (8·5 million pigs, or about two per inhabitant), and Denmark is, accordingly, the unrivalled leader in the export of bacon (particularly to the UK).

Dairy-produce has for decades been more important than meat, but export difficulties have forced the farmers, increasingly, to emphasize the production of meat. However, butter and cheese are still very important items in the Danish export, though meat export is increasing rapidly.

Eggs used to be a well-known Danish export, but since the UK introduced a protectionist policy in poultry and eggs the Danish export has lost its importance; now chickens dominate the export market in poultry produce.

Forestry

With the small forested area only a fraction of the supply of timber products is of Danish origin. The relatively highly developed furniture and paper industries are, therefore, heavily dependent on imports.

Fisheries

The shallow waters near the Danish coast are rich in fish, herring, plaice, and cod being the most important. Many North Sea harbours engage vigorously in fishing and the fishing industries. Esbjerg, Hirtshals, and Skagen are the most outstanding among them.

An increasing part of the catch is landed directly in British harbours (*e.g.*, Grimsby), and generally 50% of the total catch is exported, especially to tropical countries in Africa and Latin America.

Mining

Danish rocks are poor in minerals. Peat and low-quality lignite have been exploited during war-time but are normally unimportant. Clay, limestone, chalk, sand, and gravel occur abundantly, and bricks, cement, and mortar are the most important products based on them.

Industry

Only a minor part of the manufacturing industry is supplied by Danish raw materials. Import of fuel and a big variety of raw materials is, therefore, of crucial importance. Manufacturing of machinery, ships, foodstuffs, beverages, furniture, and chemicals are the best-known branches, all of them producing a surplus for export. Oil refining and petro-chemical industries are new in Denmark; refineries are established near the deepwater harbours of Kalundborg, Stigsnaes, and Fredericia.

More than one-third of Danish industry is located in Copenhagen, which houses the great majority of the big enterprises in shipbuilding, machine construction, brewing, etc. Textiles and foodstuffs are generally produced in small factories scattered all over Denmark, with a concentration of textile industries in the middle of Jutland, in and around the busy new town of Herning.

Danish industry has emphasized high quality more than mass production, wages are high, and the products can therefore compete only in the wealthier parts of the world; Scandinavia, Western Europe, the USA, and the USSR are, accordingly, the main customers.

Foreign Trade

With its complete lack of fuel, ores, and many other raw materials and its highly specialized agriculture and industry, Denmark must depend on a highly developed foreign trade. In spite of its small population Denmark is among the fifteen leading countries in foreign trade, and per habitant exceeded by only five countries. Manufactured products account for about 60% of the export (machines alone 20%), while agriculture contributes 35% (bacon, meat, butter, and cheese). Among imports, fuel, raw materials, foodstuffs, and machinery and vehicles are important. The main trading partners are Western Germany, the UK, Sweden, and the USA.

Imports are always of much higher value than exports; the balance is paid by the income from the merchant fleet, tourism, and Danish enterprises abroad. Denmark is a member of EFTA.

Communications

Owing to the insular character of Denmark, land and sea traffic are of equal importance. A special feature is the great number of bridges, the longest among them being the Storstrøm Bridge (3200 m., one of the longest in Europe). A dense network of motor roads makes all points easily accessible, and many international railway routes cross Denmark. SAS (the Scandinavian Airlines System) is among the biggest airline companies and competes successfully in world-wide traffic. On the Polar route SAS was a pioneer.

GREENLAND (2·2 million sq. km., with approximately 40,000 inhabitants) is the largest island in the world. Up to 1953 it was administered as a colony, but is now an integral part of Denmark, with two representatives in the Danish parliament (Folketinget). Fishing, hunting, and the processing of fish are the leading industries, but large investments are necessary in order to reach a satisfactory standard of living.

THE FAROE ISLANDS are situated in the Atlantic, far from Denmark. The population (35,000) is almost exclusively dependent on fishing and sheep-rearing. The Faroe Islands constitute a self-governing part of Denmark.

RICHARD FREDERIKSEN
Headmaster, Taarnby Secondary School
Kastrup

FEDERAL REPUBLIC OF GERMANY

[*Some Suggestions for the Presentation of
Germany in Foreign Geography Textbooks and Maps*

Today Germany is a divided country. The German Reich having
been divided into zones of occupation at the end of the Second
World War for the purpose of occupation, different political systems
emerged on either side of the demarcation line as a result of the
'Cold War' between East and West. They are the Federal Republic
of Germany in the West, and the German Democratic Republic
(GDR) in the East. This division is the root of the present German
problem.

The Four Powers—*i.e.*, the United States of America, the Soviet
Union, Great Britain, and France—made their post-war agreements
on the basis of the unity of Germany. By virtue of those agreements,
they continue to bear special responsibility for Germany as a whole.
Although the East–West conflict has meanwhile lost some of its
acute tension, the responsible Powers have so far not been able to
agree on a solution to the German problem. A final settlement by
means of a peace treaty for Germany is still outstanding.

This is the situation on which the following contribution is based.
It begins with a description of the physical geography of Germany,
devotes its main part to the Federal Republic of Germany, and then
gives a survey of the other part of Germany, the German Democratic
Republic or GDR. A final section deals briefly with those parts of
the German Reich on the other side of the Oder-Neisse line
whose destiny, according to the Four-Power agreements, is subject
to final settlement in a peace treaty.]

PHYSICAL GEOGRAPHY

Germany's physical features fall into the following natural zones:

(A) *North German Lowland*
   I. Southern Baltic coasts and lake plains.
  II. Central Elbe-Oder plain in the region of the glacial valleys.
 III. Southern heights (Lüneburger Heide, Altmark, Fläming,
      Lusatian and Silesian heights).

   IV. North-west German Lowland (Rhine-Weser-Elbe lowland).

    V. Lowland bays on the northern edge of the central mountainous uplands (Rhenish, Westphalian, Saxon, and Silesian Bays).

(B) *The Central German Mountainous Uplands (Hercynian Central Europe)*
     I. Rhenish schistous uplands.
    II. Hessian and Weser-Leine hills.
  III. Harz Mountains.
   IV. Thuringian basin with adjacent plateaux.
    V. Bohemian Forest (Upper Palatinate and Bavarian Forest).
   VI. Thuringian-Saxon uplands with the Thuringian and Franconian Forests, the Vogtland, Fichtelgebirge, Erzgebirge, Elbsandsteingebirge ("Saxon Switzerland"), Lusatian Hills.
  VII. Upper Silesian Plateau.

(C) *South German Scarplands and Mountains*
     I. Scarplands and mountains west of the Upper Rhine (German part with the Saar-Nahe highland and the Westrich).
    II. Upper Rhine valley with adjacent mountains (Black Forest, Palatinate Forest, Odenwald, and Spessart).
  III. Scarplands and mountains east of the Upper Rhine or the Swabian-Franconian scarplands including the Swabian-Franconian Alb.
   IV. Upper Main and Upper Palatinate Hills.

(D) *The Alpine Region*
     I. South German Alpine Foreland, also Swabian-Bavarian or Upper German Plateau.
    II. The Alps (German part)
       1. Swabian-Upper Bavarian pre-Alps.
       2. Northern limestone Alps with the German parts: Allgäu Alps, Bavarian Alps (Wetterstein and Karwendel Mountains), and the Berchtesgaden Alps.

The geological structure can be summarized as follows:

  (*a*) Germany consists of a number of very diverse zones tending west–east and clustered together in a relatively confined space. In them are to be found nearly all the geological formations of Europe.

(b) Large parts of Germany (North German Lowland and the Alpine Foreland) are covered by glacial deposits formed mainly by inland ice and snowmelt.

(c) The Central German mountainous uplands are composed primarily of folded crystalline Palaeozoic rocks with an intricate tectonic structure and sharply contrasting relief, the main features of which are dissected plateaux (peneplains on old folded basements), ridges, horsts, and basins.

(d) In the South German scarplands layers of Mesozoic rock form extensive plains separated by scarps. The southern faulting zone of the Upper Rhine rift valley with its adjacent mountain ridges divides the scarplands into two sections, one on each bank of the Upper Rhine.

Germany's geographical position in Central Europe governs its climate, the most prominent features of which are the frequent fluctuations of annual, seasonal, and even daily weather. It is intermediate between the oceanic and the continental climates. Three types of climate dominate: a humid temperate climate in the west, with mild temperatures and dry conditions in the basins and valleys, favourable to fruit and vine-growing, especially in the upper and middle reaches of the Rhine; a moderately humid climate in the east, with warm summer temperatures and cold to boreal climate in winter; and lastly the cold, humid mountain climate.

THE FEDERAL REPUBLIC OF GERMANY

Population

Only the Federal Republic of Germany has retained the former administrative division of Germany into *Länder*. There are altogether eleven of them, including West Berlin: the eight states of Bavaria, Baden-Württemberg, Rhineland-Palatinate, Saarland, Hesse, North Rhine/Westphalia, Lower Saxony, and Schleswig Holstein, and the three city-states of Bremen, Hamburg, and Berlin. As Berlin could not function as a capital owing to the division of Germany, Bonn became the provisional capital of the Federal Republic of Germany.

The size, density, and distribution of the population cannot be properly understood without some knowledge of the transformation of Germany from an agricultural to an industrial state since the middle of the nineteenth century, and of the expulsion and flight of almost 20 million Germans since 1945, factors which have fundamentally changed the picture of the geographical spread of the German nation in Central Europe. At present the Federal Republic of Germany has a population of 60 million in an area of 248,000 sq. km. (240 inhabitants per sq. km.). Here the population increased from 43 million to 60 million between 1939 and 1969, the latter figure including 13·2 million expellees and refugees (22% of the total population). The average excess of births between the years 1964 and 1969 was almost 7%. Every year some 60,000 Germans emigrate.

In Germany, as in other countries, the population is by no means evenly spread over the whole country. In the Federal Republic of Germany there are ten urban agglomerations, the largest being the Rhenish-Westphalian industrial region. The others are the Rhine-Main and Rhine-Neckar industrial districts, the industrial corridor along the middle reaches of the Neckar, the industrial areas of Lower Saxony, and around West Berlin, Munich, Nuremberg, Hamburg, and Bremen.

The Federal Republic of Germany has 58 cities (37 in 1939) with over 100,000 inhabitants, including 12 with over 500,000 inhabitants and 3 which exceed the million mark (Munich, Hamburg, West Berlin). These cities account for 35% of the total population. Whereas some areas have a population density of over 200, and sometimes as much as 500, inhabitants per sq. km., some of the thinly populated areas have less than 100, and sometimes even less than 50, inhabitants per sq. km. These are usually areas with unfavourable natural conditions, such as the mountainous uplands and former moorland areas which have little industrial settlement and where farming and forestry predominate.

The types of settlement in Germany can frequently be traced back to the original settlements of the Middle Ages, both in urban and rural districts; indeed the old types of houses are still to be found. The industrial revolution in the nineteenth century brought new concepts of housing and settlement, which today are discernible almost everywhere in houses on the periphery of cities and villages, and which are clearly distinct from the old forms. One striking development is the appearance of urban-type housing in villages.

The present denominational composition of the German people is the result of the nation's historical development. Prior to 1945 the pattern had changed as a result of the Reformation in 1517, the Peace of Augsburg in 1555, and the territorial dismemberment of the German Reich in 1806. After 1945 the picture changed again in the

Federal Republic of Germany owing to the influx of refugees and expellees (51 % Protestants, 44 % Catholics).

The Economy

The intensification and rationalization of the agricultural sector that gathered momentum in the Federal Republic of Germany after 1945 were originally a consequence of the War, but after 1958 increasingly so of the Federal Republic's membership of the European Community (establishment of the common agricultural market). Today the principal developments in this process are the reallocation of land, the build-up of farm holdings, resettlement, and mechanization. As the result of all these measures, the number of agricultural holdings has decreased from almost 2 million in 1949 to about 1·4 million, a reduction of 30 %. However, only 35 % of all farms can be regarded as full-time establishments (22 % are so small as to necessitate additional income while 43 % are run in addition to full-time jobs). There are very few big landowners. Of the 600,000 or so reallocated farms, over 90 % were small part-time establishments of between 0·5 and 5 hectares, most of which were not viable. But as all the measures taken to adjust agriculture to present-day conditions, especially as regards income, have proved inadequate in spite of the formation of agricultural co-operatives, a law on agriculture was promulgated in 1955, the popular name of which is the "Green Plan". The purpose of this law was to improve the economic basis of the rural population, in other words, to reduce costs, raise profits, and in general to make farm holdings competitive. Where, in 1939, 27 % of the working population were employed in agriculture, it was only 10 % in 1969. Approximately 58 % of the land used for economic purposes in the Federal Republic of Germany is concerned with agriculture and about 28 % with forestry.

Germany is one of the world's leading producers of agricultural products. The Federal Republic of Germany is the third largest producer of rye and potatoes, and the fourth largest producer of sugar beet. It is the fifth largest pig-breeding country, occupies sixth place in oats and barley production, tenth place for wheat, and thirteenth for cattle-breeding. As regards the mechanization of agriculture it occupies third place.

Industrial reconstruction and development after 1945 was the result of private enterprise and assistance from the State. The Rhenish-Westphalian industrial agglomeration with the Ruhr as its centre is Germany's largest industrial area and is one of the biggest in the world. Nowhere in Germany is there such a densely populated area and such a concentration and variety of industry as in this cluster of urban centres including 21 cities. No other part of Germany has experienced such a complete transformation from an agricultural to an industrial landscape. The bases for this development were the hard and soft coal industry and, in the nineteenth century, the iron-ore industry as well.

Today hard coal has to be mined on an average up to 760 m. below ground level. Mining is particularly difficult, since the seams of coal are usually not more than one metre thick and show considerable faulting.

The deep-mined soft coal in the areas west of Cologne is partly turned into briquettes and partly supplied to electricity works. But whereas in 1960 82% of the electric power supply in the Federal Republic of Germany came from both hard and soft coal, today only 73% comes from that source. On the other hand the use of oil for this purpose has increased from 3% to 12%. Gas, especially natural gas, and nuclear energy are also making inroads on what was once the prerogative of the coalmining industry. Taking energy consumption as a whole, the declining importance of coal becomes even more apparent, the proportion of coal used falling from 50% to 29% with a corresponding increase in oil consumption during the same period. The Federal Republic is the fifth largest electricity-producing country in the world.

The Rhenish-Westphalian industrial area yields not only 87% (80% in the Ruhr alone) of hard coal and 86% of the brown coal produced in the Federal Republic of Germany, but also 80% of the pig-iron and raw steel. The smelting of non-ferrous metals is almost exclusively confined to the Ruhr. But while the Federal Republic is not dependent on foreign supplies of hard and soft coal and also potash, it has to import over 80% of its iron-ores, almost 100% of most non-ferrous metals, and more than 90% of its mineral oil. In world production the Federal Republic of Germany ranks sixth for hard coal, third for brown coal, second for potash, and fourth for pig-iron and raw steel.

South of the Ruhr lie the centres of the hardware industry; north of the Ruhr, adjacent to the coalmines and foundries, are to be found not only the heavy industries with steelworks and rolling-mills, steel construction, mechanical engineering, and vehicle construction, but also chemical basic materials industries; along the Rhine are to be found the chemical processing plants, while the Wupper and the area west of the Rhine is the home of the textile industry. Germany is the fourth largest chemical-producing country in the world.

Other important industrial districts in the Federal Republic of Germany:

The Saarland, with coalmines, ironworks, and heavy industries.

Lower Saxon industrial district with iron-ore deposits, ironworks and heavy industries, oil and natural-gas wells, potash and salt mines, chemical industries, and the Volkswagen works at Wolfsburg.

The Rhine-Main and Rhine-Neckar industrial districts with mechanical engineering, vehicle production, chemical, and processing industries.

The industrial corridor along the middle reaches of the Neckar with predominantly processing industries (vehicle construction, electronics, chemicals, optical and precision instruments).

The Upper Bavarian industrial triangle between the Inn and Salzach rivers, with oil and natural-gas fields, chemical, and electronics industries (as in the Lower Saxon industrial district, some of these industries emerged only after 1945).

The industrial centres of Munich, Würzburg, Bremen, Hamburg, and West Berlin (mechanical engineering, vehicle, chemical, textile, and processing industries).

Most German industries are processing and refining plants, sometimes covering wide areas. They are often to be found in pronouncedly rural as well as upland regions.

Since 1945, extensive co-ordinated industrial systems have emerged in the Federal Republic of Germany; pipeline systems for water, gas, and oil, overland cables for electric-power supply.

The working population in the Federal Republic numbers approximately 27 million, 35% of these being women. Of these 27 million about 6 million are commuters and 1·6 million are foreign workers.

Trade and Traffic

Forty per cent of the long-distance goods traffic of the Federal Republic of Germany is conveyed by rail, 25% by inland waterways, 16% by road, 12% by sea, and 7% by pipelines, which are at present being considerably extended. Lufthansa (Germany's national airline) operates a network of services that spans the entire globe. About 15 million motor-vehicles, including 11 million cars, are registered in the Federal Republic. Among the world's inland waterways, the Rhine is second only to the St Lawrence River as regards the volume

F

of barge traffic and goods transport. With 6 million gross registered tons, the Federal Republic's merchant fleet ranks ninth in world trade tonnage and moreover commands an important fishing fleet. Bremen and Hamburg are among Europe's major ports, while Wilhelmshaven is an important oil transshipment port. The North Sea ports of Rotterdam (Europort) and Antwerp are important for German transoceanic traffic, while for oil supplies the Mediterranean ports of Marseilles, Genoa, and Trieste are used in addition to Rotterdam and Wilhelmshaven. Hamburg, Bremen, and Kiel have excellent shipyards which have made the Federal Republic the fourth largest shipbuilding nation.

The division of Germany since 1945 and the lowering of the 'Iron Curtain' led to a drastic disruption of all traffic by road, waterway, and air, both along the demarcation line between the Federal Republic of Germany and the GDR and along the demarcation line and sector boundary surrounding West Berlin (the Wall). Whilst before 1945 traffic currents in Germany ran mainly from west to east, the majority of them now tend south–north. Along the demarcation line between Lübeck and Hof, 34 out of 42 railway lines and 325 out of 330 roads have had to be closed. Only three air corridors are available for air traffic to West Berlin; the only two waterways, which were also available before 1945, the Elbe and the Central Canal (Mittellandkanal), are still open. The Federal Republic of Germany is the second largest trading nation in the world (after the USA) and the fourth largest industrial country (after the USA, the Soviet Union, and Japan). Its foreign trade accounts for almost a third of the gross national product. In 1968 almost 40% of the total volume of trade was transacted with the EEC countries, approximately 20% with EFTA, and roughly 10% with the United States. Among the ten most important trading partners there are nine European countries, which include all EEC members, and the USA. Finished products are the Federal Republic's main imports and exports, accounting for 45% and 85% respectively; other major imports are foodstuffs (25%) and raw materials and semi-finished products (15% each).

The exchange of goods with the GDR, commonly known as interzonal trade, accounts for just over 1% of the Federal Republic's trade volume, thus making the GDR the Federal Republic's twelfth largest trading partner.

The Federal Republic of Germany is a member of the EEC, the European Coal and Steel Community, EURATOM, the Council of Europe, and OECD; it is also a member of all specialized agencies of the United Nations. It plays a large part in the field of development aid, being the world's third largest contributor.

THE OTHER PART OF GERMANY: THE GERMAN DEMOCRATIC REPUBLIC OR GDR

In 1952, the five *Länder* of the GDR, Mecklenburg-Pomerania, Brandenburg, Saxony-Anhalt (Sachsen-Anhalt), Thuringia, and Saxony (Sachsen), were transformed into 14 regions, while East Berlin was given an equal standing as the capital and fifteenth region. At present 17·1 million Germans live in an area of 108,000 sq. km. (158 per sq. km.); in 1939 the figure was 16·7 million. About 2·8 million or 16% of the population are expellees. The average excess of the birth rate during the period 1964–68 was approximately 3·5%. The Constitution of the GDR makes no provision for freedom of movement. Only in very few cases do its authorities permit emigration.

The Saxon-Thuringian industrial district is a vast agglomeration comprising, as in 1939, 11 big cities, three with over 500,000 inhabitants and one, East Berlin, having more than one million. Together they account for 21% of the GDR population. Vast expanses, mainly between the Elbe and the Oder-Neisse line, are thinly populated (less than 100 inhabitants per sq. km., and sometimes even less than 50). According to the most recent reports, 59% of the population are Protestants, 8% Catholics, and 32% do not belong to any denomination.

In 1945, the numerous big estates in eastern Germany were expropriated without compensation and the collectivization of the rest of the agricultural sector was begun. In 1960, the bulk of the farmers who had been independent and hence free up to that time were forcibly collectivized. Today, 86% of all farmland belongs to agricultural co-operatives (LPGs), while 7% is people's property (VEG).

In connection with the reconstruction and development of industry after 1945, completely new conditions were created in East Germany. Industrial firms and many handicraft branches were expropriated and socialized without compensation—*i.e.* transformed into public enterprises (*volkseigene Betriebe*). Industrial production, including mining, is governed by the "Plan". As in agriculture, everything is geared to the requirements of five-year plans, with producer goods having priority over consumer goods.

The most important industrial region in the GDR is the Saxon-Thuringian industrial agglomeration. It is based on brown coal, copper ore, mineral and potash salts, and Europe's most important uranium ore deposits. Owing to lack of hard coal the GDR has become the world's biggest brown-coal producer. The chemical industries are of outstanding importance; in addition there are iron and steel works, whose blast furnaces are partly fed with carbonized lignite, mechanical engineering and textiles firms, and also processing industries. In the Lusatian region another important industrial centre emerged, after 1945, on the brown-coal base, with coal-carbonizing plants, electricity works, chemical industries, and iron and steel works. The working population in the GDR numbers 8 million, 46% of these being women.

Fifty-nine per cent of all goods are conveyed by rail, 37% by road, 3% by inland waterway, and 1% by sea; the pipeline system is still under construction. The transport efficiency of the railway is very considerable; 3·5 million motor-vehicles are registered in the GDR, 0·6 million of them passenger cars and 2 million motor-cycles. The merchant fleet comprises 1 million gross registered tons; in addition there exists a considerable fishing-fleet. The port of Rostock has been developed into an important international port.

The level of production and the volume of foreign trade rank second behind the Soviet Union within the communist world. Seventy-five per cent of that trade is transacted with COMECON, of which the GDR is a member, half of it with Russia. Intra-German trade with the Federal Republic of Germany accounts for about 8% of the GDR's trade volume, which makes the Federal Republic the GDR's second largest trading partner.

THE REGIONS BEYOND THE ODER-NEISSE LINE

In the eastern regions of Germany, the old Prussian provinces of (East) Pomerania, (East) Brandenburg, Silesia, and East Prussia have, in the area under Polish administration, been replaced by *voivode's* districts whose boundaries are, however, no longer identical with those of the old provinces; the northern part of East Prussia, which is now under Soviet administration, has been made an *oblast* and placed under the authority of the Russian Socialist Federative Soviet Republic. In 1939, 9·6 million Germans inhabited an area of

114,000 sq. km. (84 per sq. km.) in the eastern regions of Germany now under Polish or Soviet administration. Today the figure is 8·8 million inhabitants, 7·5 million of them Poles, 0·8 million Germans, and 0·5 million Russians. This has also produced a basic change in the denominational pattern; in 1939 66% were Protestants, 31% Catholics. The Poles and Germans now residing in those regions are almost exclusively Catholic, the Russians Orthodox, the proportion of Protestants being about 1% at the most.

The Germans in the eastern regions of Germany, as in Poland itself, were dispossessed completely and without compensation, and the majority of them were expelled. In the northern part of East Prussia where there has been an influx of Russians, the farmland is being exploited in *sovkhozes* and *kolkhozes*, whereas in the regions under Polish administration most of the land is being cultivated by small private holdings; however, the Polish settlers at present managing the land have become owners of the farms, although they have not yet been entered as such in the land registers.

The Upper Silesian industrial district, which was taken over by the Poles in 1945 in an almost completely undamaged condition, is the oldest industrial district of the European continent and was second in importance in Germany. In that district the Poles have an annual output of about 120 to 130 million tons of hard coal, which is mined at an average depth of 360 metres and in 6-metre seams; it is one of Poland's most important exports. The iron-ore deposits are now depleted; most of the ores required for smelting plants, ironworks, and steel mills are imported. The machinery and chemical industries are also important. In some areas new industrial plants have been established since 1945.

The Poles use Stettin (Szezecin), like Danzig (Gdánsk), as an overseas port, whilst the Soviet Union has developed Königsberg into a key naval port.

FINLAND

Situation

Finland is one of the most northerly countries in the world. Its southern coast roughly follows 60°N., much farther north than the southern coasts of Norway or Sweden. The territory of Finland extends in the north to 70°N. Only Norway reaches farther towards the pole. The situation of Finland could be compared with that of Iceland, but, owing to its greater north-south extent, the contrasts between the south, centre, and north are much greater than in Iceland. There are, of course, also other differences.

Physical

Finland is mainly a lowland with innumerable small hills. The terrain of Finland is in detail very varied, but the same monotonous landscape of lowlands and small hills continues through the whole country from west to east, from south to north. Only in Lapland is there found a more contrasted relief, with hills reaching a relative height of over 400 m. and an absolute elevation of 600 to 1200 m.

During the last Glacial Period the whole country was covered by a continental ice-sheet, which swept away the débris from hollows and fissures in the bedrock, also rounding and smoothing the basins of Finland's thousand lakes. When the ice-sheet melted it left behind it a layer of moraine, interrupted in places by wide stretches of sand, deposited at the edge of the ice-sheet in the water of the Baltic, and by long ridges of gravel, deposited by meltwater flowing in tunnels under the ice-sheet.

There are about 60,000 bigger and smaller lakes in Finland, the largest being Saimaa, Päijänne, Oulu, and Inari. The total lake area 32,000 sq. km., or 9% of the whole area of Finland, the coverage being 20% to 25% of the Finnish lake plateau.

The main rivers are Vuoksi, Kymi, Likemäki, Oulu, Kemi (500 km., the longest one), and Tornio.

The Climate

This represents an intermediate form between a maritime and a continental climate, being milder than most other places in the world between 60° and 70°N.; this results from the nearness of the

Gulf Stream and the prevalent western and south-western winds from the Atlantic Ocean.

The mean temperatures are:

July: South Finland +17°C., North Finland +13°C.
Feb.: South Finland −3°C., North Finland −15°C.

The annual precipitation is:

South Finland: 700 mm.
North Finland: 400 mm.

Snow covers the country for:

South Finland: 3 to 5 months.
North Finland: 7 to 8 months.

The sun is to be seen for 24 hours a day at midsummer at Rovaniemi, and the number of such days increases towards the north to 73 days in Utsjoki, situated on the Norwegian border, where during the winter the sun does not rise for 51 days.

Vegetation

Finland is a land of large forests and of very snowy winters, being part of the northern coniferous belt. The main trees are pine, spruce, and birch. In the coniferous forests there is frequently an intermixture of birch, aspen birch, aspen, and alder, and in the south even broadleaved deciduous trees like oak, lime, ash, elm, and maple. Seventy-one per cent of the total area of Finland is covered by forests, and the rest of the area is made up of 9% arable lands, 4% natural meadows, and 16% waste land.

The Finnish People

The Finns are of pure Europidic race, represented by two sub-races, the Northern and the East Baltic. Eighty-six per cent of the males and 81% of the females have blue eyes, the percentages of fair or light-brown hair being 76 and 82. The majority of the inhabitants speak Finnish. Swedish is today spoken by about 7·4%; there are only 1300 Lapps.

The Finnish language is not Indo-European, but belongs to the Finno-Ugrian group of languages. In Finnish there are many German and Russian loan words.

In 1964 about half of the population of Finland lived in towns and urban agglomerations (in 1850 only 6·4%, in 1960 40%); this indicates the very rapid industrialization of the country.

ECONOMIC LIFE

(a) Farming

Today this provides work for 31% of the population, industry 32%, and other occupations (commerce, transport, etc.) the remainder. Since the Second World War farming has been to a very great extent mechanized (from 1945 to 1964: tractors 3000 to 120,000, milking machines 0 to 45,000, combines 0 to to 20,000, etc.).

The main cereals are (crops 1962 in million kg.) oats (616), wheat (422), barley (270), and rye (101); the crop of potatoes was in the same year 950 million kg. In the southern part of the country sugar beet, peas, and rape seed are grown. The majority of the holdings are small, the arable area being 2–25 ha., but in addition the farmer usually has a considerable area of woodland (in the southern part of the country 5–6 times, in the northern part often 10–20 times, larger than the arable area) and gets from it a considerable cash income.

(b) The Forest Area

Finland has the third largest forest area in Europe (after the USSR and Sweden). Calculated per capita, Finland is richer in forest than any other country of Europe. The majority of the forests are privately owned; a considerable number, however, are owned by the State, companies, parishes, and communes. The pulp and paper industry has in recent times expanded so fast that for many years now the consumption has exceeded the growth. One of the most serious concerns of the Finnish Forestry Department is the increasing of the productivity of the forests through replanting and through the draining of boglands.

(c) Industry

Since the Second World War industry has expanded very rapidly and its structure has changed. The sawmills and pulp and paper industries have, according to the most recent data, been replaced by the metal-working and machinery industries as the most productive element in Finnish manufacture. As a result of recent construction work, the mills now have modern equipment and a modern layout.

A great part of the raw materials of the metal-working and the engineering mills is today of domestic origin (copper from Outo-kumpu and Pyhä salmi, iron from Otanmäki, Jussarö, Misi, and Raavaara, titanium from Otanmäki, vanadium from Otanmäki, zinc and lead from Vihanti, nickel from Kotasalmi). Textile, chemical, and food industries are also rapidly expanding. Finland has no coal or oil, but the majority of the Finnish rivers are harnessed to serve industry. Already 55% of all utilizable water-power is in use. The main hydro-electric stations are on the following rivers: Vuoksi, Kymi, Oulu, and especially Kemi.

(d) *The Exports*

The exports of Finland are today mainly (92%) industrial products. The main part comes from the pulp and paper factories (47% in 1963) and wood industries (22·1% in 1963)—*e.g.*, timber, prefabricated houses, plywoods, hardboards, etc. The metal-working and engineering mills (16% of the export value in 1963) produced pulp-and paper-mill equipment, tractors, locomotives, ships, railway carriages, electrical machines, cable products, etc. The chief buyers are Western European countries (especially the United Kingdom), the USSR, and South American states.

(e) *Transport*

The Finnish railway network is of a considerable density and is expanding yearly. High roads of the turnpike type have been built with permanent surfaces, while most of the other principal roads have oil-gravel surfaces, and a diminishing part of the road net is made up of gravel roads. Frost and thaw is a great enemy to roads, especially every spring, when for weeks traffic restrictions are maintained on a large number of the gravel roads. During the winter the main part of the road net is kept free from snow, a matter of necessity as the milk must be carried to the dairy centres all the year round.

Air transport is very important in Finland. There are domestic air routes. The foreign connections of the Finnish air companies include routes to Scandinavia, Central and Southern Europe, and the USSR.

(f) *The Standard of Living*

Finland has, on average, a high standard of living. Almost every family has a radio and a television set, and the TV network has been extended to include even the most remote parts of Lapland.

ADMINISTRATION

Finland is a republic, administration and social institutions of which are based on the old notion of freedom and responsibility, as in the other Norden countries (Denmark, Iceland, Norway, and Sweden). Finnish and Swedish are the official languages of the country.

The chief towns (population on 1/1/1964)

(*a*) Helsinki/Helsingfors (488,000), capital of the country. University, technical university, two universities of Economics (Finnish and Swedish), numerous public, secondary, and vocational schools. The most important site of industry and commerce in Finland. The harbour is kept open in winter by ice-breakers, as in all the southern coastal towns of Finland.

(*b*) Tampere/Tammerfors (136,300), the most important site of industry on the Western Lake Plateau. University of social sciences.

(*c*) Turku/Abo (134,800) the oldest city of the country. Former capital. Two private universities (Finnish and Swedish), important industry and commerce.

(*d*) About the other towns see *Facts about Finland* (1964).

L. A. P. POIJARVI

PROFESSOR SMEDS (deceased)
*Department of Geography
Helsinki University*

FRANCE

Naturally, textbooks on European or world geography give comparatively little space to France. The best possible use must therefore be made of those few pages in order to describe accurately the salient features of present-day France.

For pupils of 12 to 15 years it is better not to divide France into a series of regions of which the author cannot give a true and vivid picture in so little space. As a rule, in such cases, a description by regions is confined to a mere listing of facts and names.

What gives regional geography its value and justification is that it provides a synthesis, making it possible to explain the connections between facts concerning contours, climate, population, production, and trade, and to fulfil the most important aim of geography—to localize, describe, explain, and compare the different types of landscape and man's activities on the earth's surface. Regional geography requires space and time, and calls for study by minds already capable of synthesizing. It should thus be reserved for senior pupils.

The space gained by excluding regional descriptions should be used to recount actual developments in the social and economic life of modern France. In order to be of interest in this respect, a textbook should not content itself with just a few lines, and even less with more or less out-of-date generalizations. It is curious to note that agriculture predominates over industry in France, so that we appear to be dealing with a nation of farmers rather than of industrial workers; farmers, however, represent only 17% of the working population, and agriculture only 9% of the French national income (whereas industry represents 40% of the population and 53% of the national income).

This account will therefore stress what should be said rather than what is actually said in most textbooks.

I. PHYSICAL GEOGRAPHY

1. France's physical features are usually presented as follows:

The Massif Central is placed in the centre; a first concentric circle is then drawn consisting of the Paris Basin, the Aquitaine Basin, and the Rhône Valley; then a second concentric circle is drawn, on the periphery of which is placed the Massif Armoricain, the Pyrenees, the Alps, the Jura, the Vosges, and the Ardennes. This has the disadvantage of making the Massif Central the heart of France, whereas it is a region where rivers and human beings are widely scattered. The true heart of France is in the Paris Basin, or, to be even more accurate, in the Paris region. A further disadvantage is that regions as different as the Massif Armoricain and the Ardennes, the Vosges, the Jura, the Alps, and the Pyrenees are all mixed together in the outer circle. The plain of Alsace is left out altogether.

It is better to make clear that:

(a) In most of the north and west, two-thirds of the country, France has fairly low contours with plains, hills, and low plateaux; in the south and east, however, one-third of France is mountainous with rugged scenery.

(b) There is a Hercynian region of France (Massif Armoricain, Massif Central, Vosges, and Ardennes) surrounding the sunken region of the Paris sedimentary basin; a French Alpine region on the outer periphery (Pyrenees, Alps, and Jura); and a region of plains between the massifs and the mountain ranges—Aquitaine Basin, Rhône Valley, plain of Alsace.

(c) In the west of France the main lines of the Hercynian chain predominate, particularly the Massif Armoricain (direction north-west/south-east). In the east the north/south line of the Alps predominates; in the south the east/west line of the Pyrenees.

(d) No mountain range constitutes an insuperable barrier to communications. From the Paris Basin there is access to the Aquitaine Basin through the Poitou gap, from the Paris Basin to the Rhône Valley through the Burgundy gap, from the Aquitaine Basin to the Rhône Valley through the Naurouze gap. In our own day the railway and the motor-car have overcome contours and can cross the Massif Central. The highest mountains (Pyrenees, Alps, Jura) are on the country's borders. In the north and north-east France is wide open to Belgium and Germany; there lie the invasion routes but also the trade routes.

2. Apart from the Mediterranean region, confined to the Eastern Pyrenees, the Cévennes, and the Provençal Alps, France has a mainly

oceanic climate. Continental influences are apparent only from time
to time in the east, where the days are hotter in summer and colder
in winter. Rain from the sea is more frequent, on account of the
altitude, in the Limousin, the Massif Central and, farther east, in
the Paris Basin.

3. The rivers and streams are relatively small. Because of the limited
size of the country they are not as long as the great rivers of Central
Europe (Rhine, Danube) and Eastern Europe (Volga). As a result of
the oceanic climate their flow is moderate; the waters rise in autumn
and winter and fall in summer.

The Seine (776 km.), the most regular and most navigable of
the French rivers, lies throughout its course in the Paris Basin.

The Loire (1012 km.), the most irregular river, is, almost as far
as its estuary, a mountain river fed by the streams flowing down
from the Massif Central.

The Garonne (650 km.), with its estuary the Gironde, rises in the
Spanish Pyrenees and drains the Aquitaine Basin.

The Rhône (812 km.), an Alpine river, is fed by the heaviest
snows and the largest glaciers in Europe. From Lyons to the sea
it is now navigable and equipped with dams and electric power
stations.

II. HUMAN GEOGRAPHY

France has 50 million inhabitants (density 90 per sq. km).
The following should be noted:

1. The rising birth-rate since 1945 (about 18%), which increases
the population by approximately 350,000 per annum.

2. The ageing of the population owing to the decline in the
mortality rate (10·5) and the increase in life expectation (67 years for
men, 74 for women).

	1860	1954	1962 (census)
Rural population (localities of under 2000 inhabitants)	75%	46%	40%
Urban population (localities of over 2000 inhabitants)	25%	54%	60%

3. The stability of the working population, in between the young and the old: scarcely 20 million out of a population of 48 million. This gives rise to many economic and social difficulties.

4. The continued exodus from the rural areas and the rapid growth of small, medium-sized, and large towns.

5. France is still an immigration country: Algerians, Portuguese, Spaniards, and Italians come in search of work.

6. The following types of area may be distinguished:

(a) Low-density areas, with a declining population and a low birth-rate:

(i) mountainous areas;
(ii) the limestone plateaux, arid and poor, which form a semicircle from Lorraine to Poitou;
(iii) the Aquitaine Basin, which is under-industrialized.

(b) High-density areas, with a rising population and a high birth-rate:

(i) the Channel and Atlantic coasts as far as the Gironde;
(ii) the great industrial zones of the north, the northeast, the Paris basin, and the Lyons areas;
(iii) the plains of Roussillon, Languedoc, and Lower Provence, which, owing to their vines and market-garden produce, are the only highly populated agricultural regions.

III. ECONOMIC GEOGRAPHY

1. It is true that, owing to the richness of its soil, the mildness of its climate, and the ingenuity of its agricultural labourers, France is still a *largely agricultural country*. Despite its large home consumption, it can export: wheat, barley, maize, even rice; wine, fruit and vegetables; butter and cheese; meat; beet sugar. Hence its interest in the organization of agricultural markets within the Common Market.

Agricultural techniques are becoming more up-to-date; for this reason only medium and large farms or co-operative enterprises can survive. These new types of structure, which are always difficult to create, are causing profound social unrest in the farming world.

Farms	Number	Area (in hectares)
0–10 ha.	1,250,000 (56%)	6,000,000 (15%)
10–50 ha.	900,000 (40%)	19,000,000 (60%)
Over 50 ha.	95,000 (4%)	8,000,000 (25%)

2. France, however, is becoming an *increasingly industrial country*. Whereas agricultural labourers now represent 17% of the working population (26% in 1954), industrial workers represent 40%. Industry accounts for over half (53%) of the nation's wealth. Mention should be made of the substantial developments in the last twenty years of all forms of power and of industries which constitute the country's wealth—that is, iron and steel works, chemical industries, and mechanical and electrical engineering industries. France comes seventh in the world in steel, fourth in aluminium, sixth in chemical industries. It is true that France has only moderate coal resources (55 million tons a year) and practically no oil (3 million tons). On the other hand, it has a rich deposit of natural gas at Lacq, at the foot of the Pyrenees in the south-west, and a large hydro-electric energy potential in the Alps, the Pyrenees and the Massif Central, and along the banks of the Rhine and the Rhône. Lastly, France is one of the European countries richest in uranium ore (Massif Central and the Vendée).

France has built powerful thermal power-stations, as well as large oil-refining plants and petro-chemical works, in the Marseilles area (Etang de Berre), in the Seine estuary and valley between La Havre and Rouen, which is reached by the tide, in the estuaries of the Gironde and the Loire, at the port of Dunkirk, and in the Strasbourg area along the oil pipeline from Marseilles to Karlsruhe.

	1952	1966
Electricity	40 thousand million kWh.	110 thousand million kWh.
Refined oil	24 million tons	60 million tons

Thanks to the Lorraine iron-ore deposits (third in the world) France has been able to develop its iron and steel industry. This, however, is now tending to move towards the ports of arrival (Dunkirk) of iron-ore from Mauretania and coke from the United States in enormous colliers. The engineering, electrical, and electronic industries are showing rapid development.

Aluminium is extracted from bauxite, of which, thanks to the deposits in Provence, Languedoc, and the Pyrenees, France is the main European producer.

The most marked advance has been in the chemical industries. France produces large quantities of salt (both from the salt marshes of the Mediterranean coast and in the Lorraine mines), of potash in Alsace, and of natural gas, from which sulphur is extracted. Coal and oil, when chemically processed, supply numerous by-products. The chemical industries are situated in the north (coal), in the north-east (coal, salt, potash), in the Paris and Lyons regions, and at the ports.

	1952	1966
Steel	10 million tons	20 million tons
Aluminium	100,000 tons	380,000 tons
Sulphur	—	1,500,000 tons
Motor-cars	500,000	1,950,000

Of the other industries which are advancing and changing more slowly, the textile industries take first place. France still enjoys a reputation for its luxury goods (*haute couture*, leather goods, gold and silverware, crystal and glass, etc.).

3. While France lags behind as regards road and canal improvements, it has made a big effort to electrify its main railway-lines— 8500 km. out of 38,000 km., but two-thirds of its rail traffic is on those 8500 km. In terms of air traffic, Paris is second to London in Europe.

4. The big semi-public companies responsible for regional planning have begun or completed the following transformations:

(*a*) In the Landes, where there have been forest fires, the forests have been regrown, but space has been left for crops, particularly hybrid maize.

(*b*) In the south-east electrification and irrigation projects have been carried out in respect of the Durance and Rhône rivers and also navigation on the Rhône. The waters of the Rhône and Mediterranean rivers are used for irrigating the plains of Languedoc and for growing various different crops in this region which was hitherto an exclusively wine-growing area. The Durance is to supply 6 thousand million kWh. and the middle Rhône 12 thousand million kWh.

5. Lastly, various decentralization plans are being carried out. The processing industries, which are at present too densely concentrated in the Paris region, are being moved to the provinces; for instance, car factories at Le Mans and Rennes, and medium-sized factories in Normandy, the Loire Valley, etc. One of the main difficulties in making France a balanced country still lies in the shortage of industries in the west and south-east.

6. France has a planned economy, that is to say, its development proceeds according to a plan—four-year plans from 1947 to 1965 and five-year plans commencing from 1966. It is true that a large part of the economy is today nationalized (coal-mines, gas and electricity, uranium, railways and airlines, deposit banks, and insurance companies). However, private enterprise and capital are still of great importance. The Plan, which reflects the expected development of the French economy, is drawn up by those responsible (employers' federations, trade unions, civil servants).

7. France devotes approximately three thousand million francs a year to aiding the developing countries, giving priority to the French-speaking African countries and Madagascar.

L. FRANÇOIS
Inspecteur Général de l'Instruction Publique
Paris

GREECE

I. PHYSICAL GEOGRAPHY

Area

Greece has a total area of 131,944 sq. km., comprising 106,778 sq. km. on the mainland and 25,166 sq. km. of islands, of which latter only 24,909 sq. km. (169 islands and islets) are inhabited.

The country is subdivided into nine geographical regions, mainland Greece and Euboea, the Peloponnese, Thessaly, Epirus, Macedonia, Thrace, Crete, the Ionian Isles, and Aegean Islands, including the Dodecanese. Crete is the largest of the Greek islands, with an area of 8259 sq. km.

Greece is a mountainous country, 80% of its territory consisting of highlands (*cf.* France 15%, Yugoslavia 42%, Switzerland 60%). The western part has the smallest proportion of lowland.

Most of the plains are in central and northern Greece (Thessaly, Macedonia, Thrace), and the largest have the advantage of being continuous and forming a single whole (total area 10,000 sq. km. of plains ranging from 85 to 1267 sq. km.).

Rivers and Lakes

There are no major rivers in Greece. The biggest ones include the Aliakmon (285 km.) and the Acheloos (215 km.). Most Greek rivers are short, non-navigable torrents with a small flow. Use is made of some for the generation of electric power.

There are now thirteen lakes in Greece; in those not fed by permanent springs the water-level drops in summer so that they become swamps. Some of the biggest lakes in the country have been drained at various times and reclaimed for agriculture, thus increasing the area of arable land. The largest such lake is Lake Copais, with an area of 300 sq. km.

Climate

Greece has the characteristic climate shared by all countries in the Mediterranean basin. This climate, with rainy winters and long, dry summers, presents variations in the case of Greece. As one moves north the summer drought is shorter and temperatures are more extreme. Northern Greece has a climate midway between the Mediterranean climate and that of Central Europe.

The southern Aegean Islands, the Dodecanese, and Crete have a temperate maritime climate, whereas the central and northern Aegean Islands, owing to cold winds and currents, have a Mediterranean continental climate. The western coasts and the Ionian Isles have a higher rainfall than the other Greek islands.

The mountainous nature of the country means that a large part of it has a highland climate. There are variations, however, depending on latitude and the size of the massif. The main features are low temperatures and atmospheric pressure, high winds and high rainfall.

Seas

The country has a long indented coastline. The coasts are largely mountainous, with deep gulfs and innumerable promontories. The surrounding seas are dotted with islands. Out of the total length of the Greek coastline—15,021 km.—4078 km. are accounted for by mainland Greece. The island coasts are 10,943 km. in length, and are washed to the east by the Aegean Sea, to the south by the sea of Crete, and by the Ionian Sea to the west. Nowhere in Greece is the distance from the sea more than 90 km.

Flora

The flora of Greece belongs to the Mediterranean type, very rich in both deciduous and evergreen species. There are also a number of bulbs and aromatic plants.

Before being inhabited by man the whole of Greece was a vast forest. With the arrival of man primary vegetation was replaced by secondary vegetation and crops, so that nowhere today are there remaining any considerable stretches of primary vegetation.

Land use growth resulting from man's action is due to farming, sown pastures, and reafforestation.

II. HISTORICAL GEOGRAPHY AND MOVEMENTS OF POPULATION

1. *History*

In classical times Hellas was the name given to all the lands inhabited by the Greeks—*i.e.*, mainland Greece, the Peloponnese, Thessaly, Epirus, Macedonia, Thrace, the west coast of Asia Minor, Cyprus, Crete, the Aegean Islands, and the Ionian Isles. Hellenic culture left a lasting impression on Western civilization.

In A.D. 330 Constantine the Great established the new capital of the Roman Empire on the site of Byzantium, the former Greek colony of Megara. Later it was given the name of Constantinople. The Hellenization of the Eastern Empire proceeded smoothly, and the Empire subsequently became a centre of Hellenic culture and Christian teaching which spread its influence for several centuries. The Byzantine Empire was finally overcome by the last wave of Asiatic invaders, the Ottoman Turks. After the dissolution of the Empire writers, scholars, and artists who took refuge in the West made a valuable contribution to the Renaissance.

From 1830 onwards, after obtaining independence, the Greeks extended their frontiers, reconquering in turn Thessaly, Epirus, Macedonia, Western Thrace, Crete, the Ionian Isles, and the Aegean Islands.

2. *Population Dispersion and Growth*

A great many Greeks left their native land at the time of Turkish domination. But the establishment of a Greek state acted as a magnet for scattered and expatriated Greeks, and from 1839 onwards there was an increase in the population independent of the successive extensions of Greek territory.

The population of Greece is markedly homogeneous. It is almost entirely made up of people who speak Greek, and 95% of whom profess the Greek Orthodox faith.

Since 1830 the population has increased more than ten times. In 1838 it numbered 752,077, and by 1961 it was 8,388,553. The increase is accounted for not only by the widening of the country's frontiers, but by natural population growth (1931: 30·8% births compared with 17·7% deaths; 1961: 17·9% births and 7·8% deaths).

There has been a consequent increase in population density. In 1838 it was 15·8 inhabitants per sq. km., in 1861 it was 23, in 1920 36·8, in 1940 56·6, and in 1961 63·5.

3. *Emigration*

Since earliest times emigration has been a permanent social phenomenon in Greece. With remarkable energy Greeks have founded colonies throughout the world.

During the second half of the nineteenth century there were over 500,000 emigrants, mainly to the United States. The main emigration flow since the Second World War has been to West European countries. Of a total of 100,072 people emigrating in 1963, for instance, 24,459 went to Australia, Africa, and North and South America, while 75,613 went to European countries.

No less in modern than in ancient times, Greeks settling through-out the world have set up colonies which have preserved their national character intact while making a constructive contribution to life in the host countries. Such colonies are to be found mainly in the United States, Canada, Australia, Brazil, Ethiopia, South Africa, Germany, the Sudan, Egypt, and Turkey.

4. *Population Distribution*

One result of the gradual development of industry in Greece has been a change in population distribution. This change has been at the expense of the agricultural population and to the advantage of the urban population, while the semi-urban population has remained more or less static. Despite this, the country has retained its agricultural character. The farming population in 1928 represented 54·4% of the whole population, the semi-urban population 14·5%, and the urban population 31%. At the time of the 1961 census the percentages were 43·8%, 12·9%, and 43·3% respectively.

There are four major towns in Greece with a population of more than 100,000, and eight with a population of between 50,000 and 100,000. The urban centre of Athens-Piraeus has 1,832,709 inhabitants (1961). It is followed by the urban centres of Salonika (378,444) and Patras (102,244). 28·3% of the population is thus concentrated in the three largest cities.

III. ECONOMIC GEOGRAPHY

1. *Agricultural Economy*

In view of the agricultural character of the country, a series of measures has been adopted with the aim of effecting improvement, including the development of agricultural credit.

Considerable progress has been and is still being made. There are a great many shortcomings still, but it is anticipated that these will be made good by planning and by the industrialization of the farming population.

Variety in soil and weather conditions makes it possible to use modern technical methods. The administration has turned this to good account, so that the national per capita income has risen as follows: 275 dollars in 1957 and 484 dollars in 1964. An increase in private savings is also recorded.

There is no national water shortage. According to the report drawn up in 1959 in connection with the FAO Mediterranean Regional Project (MRP), water supplies represented the country's main source of wealth, after the human potential. The mountain regions with an annual mean rainfall of 1500 mm. form natural water reservoirs. Underground streams and multi-national rivers also afford considerable scope for exploitation.

Lowlands and fertile plateaux, although scattered, represent 30% of the country's total area; their soil is good and responds to modern farming techniques.

Stock-raising plays an important part in the agricultural economy. Sometimes it is nomadic, or semi-nomadic, sometimes part of settled farming.

In the last few years nomadic grazing has been on the decline. At the time of the 1962 census there were 1,157,000 head of cattle, 513,000 pigs, 8,899,000 sheep, 4,389,000 goats, 329,000 horses, 221,000 mules, and 474,000 donkeys. The main stock-rearing regions of Greece are in the north.

Poultry-rearing, bee-keeping, and silkworm-breeding make a fairly substantial contribution, though the latter two are declining.

2. *Geographical Distribution of the Staple Agricultural Products*

The main agricultural products are distributed as follows:

(*a*) cereals in the centre and north;
(*b*) citrus fruits in the centre and south and also in the Ionian Isles, the Aegean Islands, and Crete;
(*c*) olives in the centre and southern regions and also in the Ionian Isles, the Aegean Islands, and Crete;
(*d*) plants for industrial purposes in various regions depending on species;
(*e*) fruit trees other than those mentioned above, vegetables, and early fruit and vegetables also grow in various regions, according to their kind.

The most characteristic Greek agricultural products are olives, grapes, citrus and other fruits, and tobacco. Greece is the ninth largest producer of tobacco in the world, the twelfth largest producer of grapes and raisins, the third largest producer of olive oil and olives, and the eighteenth largest producer of wheat.

3. *Mountains and Seas, Forests and Fishing*

Despite the mountains and the good climate, a mere 15% of

Greek territory is forest-clad, whereas in the other Balkan countries the proportion is between 25% and 30%. Scope for afforestation is considerable, however. The main Greek forest trees are oak, pine, fir, beech, and chestnut. The biggest forests are in Thessaly, Macedonia, Thrace, central Greece, and the Peloponnese.

Forest products make only a small contribution (3·2%) to the total national agricultural production.

Nearly all the sea surrounding Greece is rich in fish. Fishing was not greatly developed before the First World War, but Turkish and Bulgarian refugees settling in Greece helped in the application of more sophisticated methods, leading to an expansion in fishing.

Atlantic fishing has also developed quite recently. In 1965 there were 34 large Atlantic-going fishing vessels, 793 big fishing vessels (deep-sea), 5817 offshore fishing vessels (all motor-powered), and 10,000 rowing-boats. The number of fishermen was 55,600. The national income from fishing amounts to almost 1% of the gross national product. Sponge-diving is also an important occupation.

4. *Industry*

Industry and skilled trades play an important part in the development of the Greek economy.

The total numbers employed in secondary industry and trades amount to 481,000, or 13·1% of the working population, with an income in 1961 of 17·8% of the gross national product.

Most of the country's industrial activity is concentrated in the urban centre of Athens-Piraeus.

There are industrial centres also at Salonika, Patras, Velos, Larissa, Cavala, and a few other towns. The main industries are textiles (24·5%), foodstuffs (17·5%), and chemicals (13%).

5. *Sources of Energy*

Greece's sources of energy are lignite and hydro-electric powei No oil has been found to date. Total reserves of lignite are put at some 900,000,000 tons. The main lignite deposits are at Ptolemais and Aliverion, where two thermal power stations are in operation.

There is extensive scope for utilizing waterfalls. At the moment a mere 0·1% of the waterfall potential is harnessed, and the hydro-electric power supplied represents 33% of the country's total electricity consumption.

The main hydro-electric power stations use water from the

Tavropos, Ladon, Agras, and Louros rivers. Electric power production totals 2940 million kWh. of which 2151 million are produced by thermal power stations and 789 million by hydro-electric power stations (1963). Under the ten-year plan electric power production is to be raised to 12,750,000,000 kWh.

6. Mineral Wealth

The rocks of Greece are rich in a wide variety of metals used in industry. Greek mineral resources can be classified under the heads of ores, mineral coal, and the products of quarries. The main ores are bauxite (1,300,000 metric tons in 1964), iron ore, magnesite, and emery. Lignite is also found (3,804,000 metric tons in 1964). There are in addition substantial veins of chromite, nickel, lead, zinc, barytes, asbestos, and manganese. The quarried products are mainly marble (44,393 cubic metres in 1962), kaolin, and sulphur.

7. A Maritime Nation

The Greeks have always felt the lure of the sea. The merchant fleet flying the Greek flag is the sixth largest in the world today (1232 vessels in 1962, with a tonnage of 6,774,000 CU–GRT). If all ships belonging to Greek shipowners, flying other flags, are included, Greece has the third largest merchant fleet in the world, with a tonnage of 20,000,000 CU-GRT.

8. Transport

The ruggedness of the country and shortage of capital are the main obstacles to the development of transport by land. The road and rail systems are not sufficiently tightly knit, and the most convenient form of transport is still by sea, particularly for heavy goods.

In 1962 the railway network extended over 2583 km. The road system has been considerably developed in the last ten years, until today there are over 32,567 km. of national and regional roads.

Civil aviation has also made considerable headway since the war. There are now eighteen civil airports in Greece, with a total of 27,689 outgoing and 27,691 incoming flights (1963).

Shipping routes provide links with otherwise inaccessible regions. The main Greek ports are Piraeus, Salonika, Patras, Velos, Corfu, Iraklion, Cavala, and Eleusis. Sea transport, internal and external, is thus used more than any other form of transport.

9. *Trade*

Recently trade has made great strides. Imports are mainly in the form of certain industrial products and agricultural produce, while exports consist mainly of agricultural produce and industrial raw materials. The main exports are tobacco (32 % of exports), raisins, olive oil, wine, grapes, fruit, cotton, and minerals.

The main supplier countries are the United States, Great Britain, West Germany, Holland, Brazil, France, and Italy. Exports go mainly to West Germany, the United States, Brazil, the Soviet Union, and Great Britain. The association of Greece with the European Common Market is opening up new avenues for Greek trade.

10. *Tourist Industry*

Greece has become a focal point for large numbers of tourists from all corners of the world, because of her climate, natural beauty, and the impressive reminders of her ancient civilization. More visitors come to Greece every year. In 1957 the number of tourists was 260,280, and by 1963 the figure had risen to 741,193. Economically speaking, the expansion of the tourist industry has helped to balance Greece's external payments.

GEORGES IVANTCHOS
Political Science Bureau
Athens

ICELAND

In many ways Iceland has an exceptional position among the other European countries. It is situated where temperate and Arctic climates meet, at the junction of forest and tundra. Placed between America and Europe, its geology and surface features are quite unlike those of either continent.

The population of Iceland does not exceed that of a middle-sized town in industrialized Europe, but its standard of living is often higher than that of bigger nations.

Position and Size

Iceland is situated between 63° 23′ N. and 66° 36′ N., just touching the Arctic Circle. It is at the crossing-point of two submarine ridges, one going from Scotland to East Greenland, the other, the N.–S. Mid-Atlantic Ridge. The area is 103,000 sq. km.

Geology

The eastern and western parts of Iceland are made up of Tertiary basalt, but the central and south-western parts are mainly of eruptives from glacial and post-glacial times, interspersed with alluvial and glacial sediments. Post-glacial volcanic activity has been limited to this central zone. Most types of volcanoes can be found among the 180 recently active volcanoes. During the past few centuries an eruption has occurred on an average every fifth year, the last one being the submarine eruption (1963 to 1967) south of Iceland, when the island Surtsey rose from the sea. Hekla, the most famous Icelandic volcano, has been built up as a result of many eruptions along its 5-km. linear eruption vent. Open fissures and lines of craters are the most common types of volcanoes in Iceland, but explosion craters, shield-volcanoes, cones, and several other types are also found.

Of the surface of Iceland about 10% is covered by post-glacial lava-fields, mostly basaltic, but rhyolite occurs in a few places. Hot-water springs are common throughout the country (in about 250 localities), but natural steam-fields (solfatara fields) are limited to the zone of post-glacial vulcanism. The thermal gradient is everywhere above the European average (0·03°C/m), lowest in the

Tertiary basaltic zone and highest in and around the steam-fields where it exceeds 1°C/m.

The Great Geyser is still the most famous among geysers, although its activity seems to be in decline. But there are several others. Practically all the greenhouses, swimming-pools, etc., and about half the living houses in Iceland are now heated by natural steam, and it is common to see the derricks, used for drilling, even inside towns. Only a very small part of the heat available has yet been tamed.

The Landscape

The major part of Iceland is a plateau, 600–800 m. above sea-level, but above it rise smaller blocks reaching 1600–2000 m., besides many volcanoes. The snowline is at about 1000 m. on the southern slopes, where precipitation is high, and the higher plateaux are thus covered by glaciers. The area of the biggest one, Vatnajökull, is about 8400 sq. km., but altogether some 11 % of the entire area is glacier-covered. From the plateau icecaps protrude many valley glaciers; some of them broaden out on the lowlands, particularly south of Vatnajökull, and a large number of glacial rivers spread out on the lower plateaux and lowlands, giving rise to sandy plains and outwash fans. Sudden floods are common in many of the glacial rivers, owing to volcanic activity beneath the glacier or to ice-barriers that suddenly burst to release the dammed up water.

Only about a fourth of the area of Iceland is under the 200-m. line. Most lowland is along the south coast. In the eastern part it is covered by sand, but there is grassland and low bushes with patches of cultivation in the west.

In the south and parts of the north, where the debris-laden glacial rivers discharge their loads, sandy coasts, reefs, and lagoons are common, and there are no harbours. In the Tertiary basaltic areas in the east and west cliffs drop steeply into the ocean on the peninsulas, but the deep fjords offer good harbours.

The Climate

The cyclones following the polar front across the North Atlantic give very unstable weather conditions in and around Iceland, and the warm North Atlantic Drift meets and mixes with the cold East-Greenland or Polar current north and west of the island. The East-Greenland current sometimes brings drift ice in winter to the north and east coasts. It may prevent ships putting out to sea and usually brings extremely low temperatures. But normally the climate is oceanic, with an average air-temperature in July of 11°–12°C. in the south, and a couple of degrees lower in the north and east; and 0°–1°C. in January in the south and −2° to −5°C. in the north and east. The average surface temperature in the surrounding ocean is in winter 4°–6°C. higher than the average air temperature, but on the other hand the ocean cools the air on warm summer days. The frontiers of the Arctic and temperate climates thus meet in Iceland.

Precipitation is high in the south, 100 to 300 cm. per year, but drops below 50 cm. in the north. The relative humidity is high, evaporation low, and there is therefore a considerable run-off of surface water.

Vegetation

About a quarter of the area is covered by some sort of vegetation, the plateaux and mountains being practically bare except for small bogs and swamps where cotton grass and sedges grow. Only about 1 % of the whole area is forested, chiefly by patches of birch, mountain ash, and several sorts of willow.

Erosion is a big problem, and large areas of farmland have been ruined in historical times.

The People

The Icelanders are of Nordic stock. They are very proud that their language has been practically unchanged for 1000 years, so that everybody can read their 900-year-old literature (The Eddas, the Sagas, etc.).

In 1967 there were 200,000 people living in Iceland: their number had more than trebled since 1890. The birth rate was very high (between 25 and 30%) up to 1965, but dropped suddenly in 1967 below 20%. The death rate has been very low, or about 7% in the last twenty years, and the average length of life, in 1951–60, was for men 71 years and for women 75.

About half of the inhabitants live in the south-west part of the country, which includes the capital, Reykjavik, and its suburbs. About four-fifths of the people live in towns and villages, and less than 20% on scattered farms in the country. Fishing ports are found in sheltered places in the fjords, and during recent decades manufacture, trade, and communication centres have been developing in the main farming districts.

Production

Animal husbandry used to be the main occupation, but now

only about 15% of the population is engaged in farming; numbers are still decreasing, but their production is increasing owing to growing mechanization, technical skill, and research. Grass and potatoes with some fodder beets are the main agricultural product. Grain scarcely grows at all owing to low summer temperatures.

The area of cultivated grassland has trebled since 1920, but there is still only a small area of arable land. In valleys and some outlying regions sheep-raising is still the main occupation, but around the towns dairy-farming is rapidly growing. People consume large quantities of milk and dairy produce in their daily food. It is common for the sheep to roam untended in the uninhabited highlands during the summer months. Usually farmers produce enough meat and dairy produce for the home market, and sometimes a surplus for export.

Fishing. About 8% of the working force is occupied in fishing and this produces annually about 1 million tons (in 1966 1·2 million tons), or a figure of 250–300 tons per fisherman, probably the highest in the world. Catches fluctuate from year to year, so the fishing industry is very unstable. Icelandic fishing-boats may now be seen all over the North Atlantic, from Great Britain to Spitsbergen and over to East Greenland and Newfoundland. Icelandic fishing-banks are possibly over exploited.

Cod and herring are usually the main fish in the catch, but often the shoals of herring fail to appear. The fishing fleet must be furnished with safe modern equipment, because weather is severe in winter in the North Atlantic. Iceland is usually among the world's fourth to sixth leading fish exporters.

Industry. About two-fifths of the working force is in manufacturing industries, with food processing easily leading, but building fishing-boats, making fishing gear, textile industries, etc., are also of importance. Centres of manufacture are in Reykjavik and its surroundings—for instance, plants for nitrogenous fertilizers, cement, and aluminium, besides shipbuilding, fish processing, and textiles—but in the last decade manufacturing has spread to other towns. In Akureyri in North Iceland, for instance, there are shipbuilding, textile and leather processing, and chemical industries. At Myvatn, farther east, the production of diatomaceous earth has just started. The herring industry is centred on the north and east coasts.

Power. Water-power is estimated at 35,000 million kWh. per year and hot water-power at perhaps the same amount. Together, these energy sources will meet the needs of 15–20 million people, using, as in 1963–64, about 3350 kWh. per year per capita. Of the water-power about 2% was utilized by 1967, but 95% of the built-up areas had electricity. By 1969 hydro-electric power production had more than doubled, most of the increase being used in the extraction of aluminium.

Trade. External trade per capita is generally the highest in Europe. More than 90% of the value of exports has been fish and fish products. Usually there is a large deficit on the balance of external trade.

Communications

There have never been railways in Iceland. In the period 1920–50 cars and aeroplanes replaced ponies and human carriers. Roads are still unsurfaced (dirt roads), but there is about 1 km. of road for each inhabitant, so the building and maintenance of roads involves a heavy expenditure. The aeroplane has largely taken over the passenger traffic, both external and on longer inland routes. The Keflavik airport in the south-west corner is the centre for air communications with Europe and America.

The merchant fleet (330 BRT per 1000 inhabitants) copes with the external transport of merchandise. Reykjavik is the main centre for trade and internal transport.

It is often said that Iceland lies at the limits of the habitable earth. In spite of that the Icelanders have been able to create a very high and evenly distributed living standard, and their national product has been rapidly growing for the last three to four decades. During that period a primitive self-sufficient farming society has changed into a highly mechanized and industrialized nation. In the last thirty years practically every stable and farmhouse has been rebuilt, concrete buildings replacing the turf houses. Roads, telephones, and electricity are taken to every farm, every family has a radio and a bath, and there is at least one car for every five inhabitants.

The Icelanders have never had any army or conscription. This may help to explain how this handful of people in hard and unyielding surroundings have a private annual consumption of more than 1500 US dollars per capita and were able to increase their real gross national product by about 6%–8% yearly in the period 1961–65.

SIGURDUR THORARINSSON
Professor of Geology and Geography University of Iceland

IRELAND

I. INTRODUCTION

(*a*) Physically Ireland is a detached fragment of the continental mainland and part of the western oceanic fringe of Europe. It lies farther north than Newfoundland, but its climate is modified by the prevailing winds which blow off the relatively warm waters of the North Atlantic drift so that the winters are relatively mild (5–7°C.) and the summers correspondingly cool (14–16°C.). These winds coming from the ocean have a high moisture content and may bring rain at any season. Total annual rainfall is highest along the west coast and on the hills (40–80 in.—1000–2000 mm.) but it is much less in the east, where Dublin receives only 27 in. (700 mm.). Sunshine and showers with mild, clear air giving visibility over great distances are the characteristic weather conditions.

(*b*) Though structurally and climatically linked with Western Europe, Ireland is socially and economically distinct from its neighbours. The farms are smaller, the towns fewer, and industry of less importance than in Great Britain or on the continental mainland. Owing to her marginal position Ireland was never conquered by the Romans, and when the neighbouring island was over-run by invaders in the early part of the Christian era, Ireland remained a Celtic Christian community with an unbroken continuity of tradition.

(*c*) Politically Ireland has been divided since 1922 into two parts. The Constitution of Ireland declares that national territory is the whole island, but that, pending its re-integration, the area of jurisdiction of the Irish Parliament and Government dealt with in this paper is restricted to 26 of the 32 counties of the island. Ireland is a sovereign independent democratic state.

II. PHYSICAL AND HUMAN GEOGRAPHY

(*a*) Emphasis should be laid on the variety of the Irish physical landscape. This results from the meeting and mingling of two of the great mountain systems of Europe (Caledonian and Hercynian) and from the effects of former glaciation which has produced most of the minor relief features of the landscape, including many mountain and lowland lakes.

Ireland is best studied at an elementary level on the basis of three main physical divisions—the Caledonian mountains of the west and south-east, the Hercynian ranges of the south, and the Central lowland. Each of these has a distinctive human response; so a note on the human geography is added immediately after a description of their physical features.

The combination of rugged mountains, lakes, and cultivated lowland is scenically very attractive, and large numbers of tourists visit Ireland every year.

(b) Caledonian Ireland

The mountains which occupy most of the counties of Donegal, Mayo, and Galway in the north-west of Ireland and the counties of Wicklow and Wexford in the south-east, are the remnants of extensive mountain ranges which once occupied most of north-west Europe. These mountains average about 1500 ft (500 m.) in height and are bare and windswept. In coastal areas they may form rugged sea cliffs, and elsewhere masses of resistant quartzite have weathered into conical peaks which rise above the general level of the countryside, such as Errigal (2466 ft, 750 m.) in Donegal, and Croagh Patrick (2510 ft, 766 m.) in Mayo. The soil is thin or absent on the upper slopes, and there is extensive peat development. Strong winds prevent tree growth except in sheltered valleys, but along the limited area of coastal lowlands and in the valleys which penetrate deep into the hills there is a dense population working small livestock farms. These farmers supplement their income by fishing, home industry, or by periodic migration to other parts of the country and to Great Britain for the harvest.

The Caledonian mountains of the east are less rugged. The main range extends south-west from Dublin Bay and is largely composed of granite. It is penetrated from the east by deep glacially modified valleys, of which Glendalough is the best known. Forests, partly natural oakwood but mostly planted conifers, clothe the lower slopes, while the higher parts are heather moorland. This is one of the most beautiful and accessible parts of Ireland.

(c) Hercynian Ireland

In the south of Ireland east-west trending hills are a western extension of Hercynian Europe. Synclinal valleys floored with limestone or shale alternate with anticlinal ridges of Devonian sandstone which become the dominant feature of the landscape in the south-west, where the Macgillycuddy's Reeks form the highest land in the country. These sandstone ridges, as rugged peninsulas stretching far out into the Atlantic Ocean, are separated by drowned river valleys, so that there is a typical ria coastline. The absence of severe frost in this part of Ireland allows the growth of sub-tropical plants, and vegetation is richer than that found farther north. However, as in the other western areas, the small livestock farm dominates. Eastwards, where the valleys widen out and the intervening hills are lower, the larger dairy farm appears and there is more arable farming. This part has its focus on Cork, the second city of the state and an important port and manufacturing centre.

(*d*) *The Central Lowland*

The greater part of Ireland is occupied by a lowland that averages less than 300 ft (100 m.) above sea-level. This lowland forms the east coast for 80 km. from Dublin northwards and reaches to the west across the centre of Ireland to the shores of the Atlantic at Limerick, Galway, Mayo, and Sligo, where, in each case, it forms broad corridors of richer land between the higher mountain masses. Much of the lowland is drained by the wide, slow-flowing river Shannon. Near Limerick the Shannon drops rapidly through 30 m. to sea-level, and it is here that the first hydro-electric scheme in Ireland was located in 1928.

The lowland is covered by glacial deposits which in the north-central part give rise to a distinctive landscape of hundreds of small steep-sided hills about 20 m. high (drumlins), which extends from Sligo in the west to Louth in the east. Elsewhere the surface forms are more subdued, but variety is provided by the extensive peat deposits (raised bogs) which are an important source of fuel for power. Most of the lowland is important agriculturally but the farmland is especially good in the south-west, in the counties of Limerick and Tipperary, and in the east around Dublin, where the large farm predominates. Dublin, the focus of routes across the lowland to the Irish Sea, is the capital, chief port, largest town, and most important industrial centre in the country.

III. POPULATION

(*a*) The state covers an area of 27,136 sq. miles (70,281 sq. km.) and in 1966 had a population of 2,884,002; this gives an average density of 106 per sq. mile (41 per sq. km.). The population density per sq. mile for the provinces is Leinster, 186·6, Munster, 92·2, Connacht, 60·8, Ulster (part of), 67·3.

(b) Ireland has had a declining population for over one hundred years because of large-scale emigration to Great Britain, the United States, and other countries overseas. The emigrants have come mainly from the rural areas and smaller towns, while the larger towns have maintained their numbers. This has meant that there is an ever-increasing proportion of the people living in urban areas. Recent population figures indicate a significant increase in the total population of the country.

IV. ECONOMIC GEOGRAPHY

Ireland's main wealth lies in the soil, which, with the mild, moist climate, favours pastureland and leads to a concentration on livestock production. There is also increasing industrial development and a rapidly growing tourist trade.

1. *Agriculture*

(a) *Land use* (1965)

Distribution of productive and and non-productive land	
Pastureland	49·7%
Hay	12·1%
Crops and fruit	7·6%
Woodland, bogs and wasteland	30·6%

Percentage of farms of different sizes	
1–30 acres (1–12 ha.)	48·2%
30–100 acres (12–40 ha.)	41·1%
100 acres + (40 ha. +)	10·7%

(b) *Livestock.* Cattle are the most important animals and number nearly 5·6 million animals, of which almost one-third are cows. Meat and milk are the principal products. Young beef cattle, raised on the smaller farms everywhere, are brought to the larger farms in the eastern lowland for fattening and export. Sheep number about 4·2 million and occur on all the hill land, but are chiefly in Donegal, Wicklow, Roscommon, and Galway. Other animals include pigs and poultry, which form an important part of the output of the smaller farms especially in the south, and thoroughbred racehorses raised on the rich pastures of Meath and Kildare.

(c) *Crops.* The chief crops are wheat, oats, barley, and root crops. Wheat is grown mainly on the larger tillage farms in the eastern part of the country. Oats are the most important crop in the west and are grown on the small farms for livestock feeding, while barley, which is grown on the large and medium-sized farms, is increasing in importance and is the main cereal crop of the south. Other important crops are turnips, potatoes, and sugar beet. The latter meets all Ireland's requirements for sugar. There is a small but significant production of fruit and vegetables.

The standard of farming has greatly improved in recent years through the activities of the agricultural advisory and educational services, grants for land drainage and fertilizers, and through increasing mechanization; the findings of research bodies such as the Agricultural Institute are being increasingly used to improve farming efficiency.

The Land Commission is engaged on a programme to secure the better distribution of land by purchasing estates for division among neighbouring small farmers. In addition many farmers from the poorer western areas are being resettled on larger and more fertile holdings in the midlands and the east. Their vacated lands are then used in the rearrangement and enlargement of other uneconomic holdings in the vicinity.

(d) *Forestry.* Ireland has few trees by European standards, but the Forestry Commission has been planting at an average rate of 25,000 acres per annum. The planting is mainly of commercial softwoods on the poorer hill lands, and this activity is changing the face of the countryside, especially in County Wicklow.

2. *Industry and Power*

(a) *Industry.* Ireland has many light industries covering an exceptionally wide variety of products. The older centres of industry are Dublin and Cork, but until recently it was Government policy to disperse new industries widely throughout the country. There is now a tendency towards concentration in the larger centres of population, with plans to create industrial estates in Galway and Waterford and to continue development at the Shannon Free Airport near Limerick. Manufacturing includes food processing, brewing, tobacco products, textiles, clothing and footwear, paper-making, metal trades, electrical equipment, and motor vehicles, etc. The increasing importance of industry as a source of employment is indicated below.

Number of Persons at Work in Main Branch of Economic Activity

	1926	1936	1946	1956	1966
			(Thousands)		
Agriculture, forestry, fishing	652	613	567	430	333
Industry	163	208	229	269	285
Other economic activities	405	414	432	426	447
Total at work	1220	1235	1228	1125	1065

(b) *Power Supply.* Electricity is available in all parts of the country from the national grid. It is produced from imported oil and coal and from water and peat. There is an oil refinery near Cork which serves the needs of the country.

Sources of Electric Power
(Percentage of power from the three sources)

	(a) 1956	(a) 1958	(a) 1961	(a) 1965	(a) 1966	(a) 1968
Coal and oil	46	31	26	43	47	54
Peat	23	30	33	33	27	27
Water	31	39	41	24	26	19

The total output in 1956(a) was 1570 million kWh.
and 4242 million kWh. in 1968(a).
(a) Year ended March 31.

3. *Communication and Trade*

(a) *Communications.* Despite its relatively low density of population, Ireland is well served by a dense network of good roads. The main towns are also linked by fast train services, though nationalization of the railway system has meant the closing of most of the branch lines. External communications are by sea and air. There are daily cross-channel services between Dublin and Liverpool, Dun Laoghaire and Holyhead, and Rosslare and Fishguard. Irish Airlines using the international airports of Dublin, Cork, and Shannon provide frequent air services with the principal cities of Great Britain and Western Europe, and with New York, Boston, Chicago, and Montreal.

(b) *External Trade.* Ireland trades principally with Great Britain and other West European countries. Outside Europe her main trade is with the United States of America. Agricultural produce, though decreasing in relative importance, is still the most important item of export.

Exports

	1954	1967
Agricultural products	62·7%	53·2%
Other exports, including manufactured articles	37·3%	46·8%

The total domestic exports in 1956 were valued at £104,276,000 and in 1967 at £275,688,000.

PROFESSOR J. P. HAUGHTON
Trinity College
Dublin

ITALY

Italy is one of the countries of Europe with a markedly individual character. It has well-defined boundaries consisting of three seas (Tyrrhenian, Adriatic, Ionian) and of the watershed of the Alpine range which divides the river systems flowing directly to the Mediterranean from those feeding the Rhône, Rhine, and Danube.

I. THE NATURAL CONDITIONS

Italy is divided into four areas possessing their own distinctive characteristics:

(1) *Alpine Italy* comprising the mountainous areas of the north, higher in the west than in the east, intersected by fairly broad, longitudinal valleys suitable for settlement (Valtellina, Val Venosta, etc.) or by transverse valleys formed by deeply-entrenched rivers, usually sparsely populated but suitable for purposes of communication across the Alps.

(2) *The Venetian lower Po* valley and the basins of the Venetian rivers flowing into the Adriatic.

(3) *Apennine Italy*, which comprises the peninsular part proper of Italy bounded by plains, particularly on the Tyrrhenian side (Lower Valdarno, Agro Romano, Agro Pontino, Campania Felice, Piana del Sele, etc.).

(4) The two big *Mediterranean islands* (Sicily and Sardinia).

Italy's main distinctive features are the following:

(1) Its position in the centre of the Mediterranean. The town of Messina, for example, is at a roughly equal distance from Gibraltar and the Suez Canal. Since ancient times Italy has had relations with the other Mediterranean countries, with which it has many features in common (climate, vegetation, manner of settlement, etc.); these features have a profound influence on the life and activity of the people.

(2) Its peninsular form rather like a pier, which facilitates contact with other countries: the Apulia area with the

Balkan region and the Levant, Sicily with North Africa.

(3) The fact that it is bounded by the great Alpine range across which there are many easily accessible and much frequented passes: communication between the northern and southern slopes has been improved by the building of a series of tunnels (Frejus, Simplon, St Gotthard, and, recently, the Mont Blanc and Great St Bernard road tunnels). Italy is therefore a European as well as a Mediterranean country.

Italy has many natural advantages:

(1) Great morphological variety: Italy is a country of plains, hills, and mountains; the permanent and manifold relations between these areas are becoming ever more numerous with the development of road traffic.

(2) A number of highly fertile plains such as the Venetian, lower Po, the Campanian, certain parts of Tuscany, Emilia, the Marches, Latium, Apulia, and Sicily.

(3) The beneficial Mediterranean influence which attenuates the harshness of the climate and permits the culture of certain subtropical products (citrus fruits). There is a very marked contrast between the areas which benefit from this favourable influence (the islands, Liguria, the Tyrrhenian, Ionian, and Adriatic coastal areas) and the inland regions (the Venetian lower Po plains, the Alpine area, and the Apennine region), where winters are very harsh and the climate resembles that of Central Europe.

Italy's *drawbacks* are:

(1) The modest area of the plains in relation to the mountainous country. Above an altitude of 800 m. in the Alps and 1000 or 1200 m. in the Apennines, agriculture is impossible. The meadows and pastures are used for stockbreeding only. Most of central and southern Italy is taken up by barren and uninhabited mountain country, as are large areas in the Alps.

(2) The relative shortness of the rivers with their irregular water systems which makes them unsuitable for

navigation; there is little irrigation, particularly in southern Italy.

(3) The many coastal marshlands, formerly malaria-ridden.

(4) The irregularity of the climate in the south (long summer droughts, sudden and destructive downpours, etc.), which often causes serious damage to agriculture.

(5) The frequent floods and landslides, particularly in Lucania and Calabria.

II. MAN'S WORK THROUGHOUT HISTORY

In the past Italy was more thickly wooded than today. In the lower regions the forest was frequently felled to make room for agriculture. Higher up the forest was reduced to permit the extension of the pastures or because the timber was needed for working-up or burning. This too rapid and irrational felling of the forest has had grave consequences: as a result of the deforestation, particularly in the Apennines, the slopes suffered accelerated erosion by torrential rains which uprooted the surface vegetation and in some places bared the rock.

The purpose of the reafforestation currently in progress is the reconstitution of the protective forest cover in the mountain areas. Reafforestation is, however, impeded by the difficulty which trees have in growing again in Mediterranean countries once they have been felled. Trees (particularly poplars) have recently been planted throughout northern Italy, even in the plains and on the hills, where agriculture was uneconomical and the area became depopulated.

Among the work accomplished by man with a view to acquiring new agricultural lands an important place is occupied by reclamation —i.e., the complicated process of the draining of marshy plains. There were formerly very extensive, unhealthy plains throughout the Po area, the lower Adige basin, and the Romagna; the greater part of these plains were drained and cultivated thanks to extensive reclamation work begun in th Middle Ages and continued up to the present day.

The intensification of drainage n the areas of central and southern Italy is even more recent. In the Abruzzi the Fucino Lake (150 sq. km.) was drained and placed under cultivation, in Tuscany the maremmas, in Latium the whole coastal area, which now abounds in farms, rural centres, and prosperous towns such as Latina, Pontinia, and Sabaudia.

Major work has also been carried out in the depressions bordering on the Gulf of Naples (lower reaches of the Volturno) and the Gulf of Salerno (Sele plain), in Lucania (Metaponto plain) and Calabria (Sibari and Sant, Eufemia plains, and other coastal areas), Apulia (Tavoliere), Sicily (Catania plain), Sardinia (Campidano, Gulf of Oristano, etc.).

The unceasing advance of the deltas of the main rivers (Po, Tiber, etc.) has, in its turn, aroused the unceasing intervention of man, who endeavours to canalize and turn aside the waters and provide them with new outlets. However, a sudden rise of the waters may cause disastrous floods and destroy the work of several centuries in a few hours, as happened in the Po delta in 1951.

Another means of reclaiming land is irrigation, necessary in a number of areas of Italy either because of summer droughts or the aridity of the permeable soil. It is only in the Venetian lower Po valley that there are abundant internal water reserves (rivers, lakes) usable for irrigation: it is there that three-quarters of Italy's irrigable lands are situated. Certain canals, including the Cavour Canal, are navigable as well as irrigable. There are far fewer irrigable areas in southern Italy and the islands where the rivers lack water, particularly in the summer. But here a number of artificial basins can also constitute irrigation reservoirs.

Another series of measures was called for by the need to co-ordinate coal and oil energy supplies with hydraulic energy resources. There are today 2325 power plants (with a capacity exceeding 13 GWh.), 1600 of which are in the Alpine area. To regulate the water-flow it was necessary to create some 600 reservoirs of artificial lakes, of which about 60 are of considerable size. They represent the most striking transformation of the Italian countryside. Most of the big lake reservoirs are situated in northern Italy, but there are also some in central Italy, three in Calabria, two in Sicily, and four in Sardinia. The landscape has often undergone radical change: narrow valleys have been turned into basins, and it has been possible to start human activity in formerly uninhabited areas.

Transformation in progress includes the major agrarian reform whereby large rural holdings are being divided up. Comfortable dwellings and the means necessary for tilling the land are made available to the peasants, to whom plots are assigned.

The economic and social development of southern Italy has been greatly aided by the creation of the *Cassa per il Mezzogiorno*, which has carried out extensive work relating to the improvement of mountainous areas, drainage, irrigation, road-building, land reform, and development of the tourist potential.

Besides the areas having undergone profound changes, there are the regions, less extensive, where the natural conditions are being preserved thanks to the forming of National Parks. There are four such parks in Italy: Gran Paradiso (Piedmont), Adamello (Tridentine Venetia), Circeo (Latium), and Abruzzi.

III. POPULATION

The Italian population has increased considerably over the last fifty years (1911: 35·8 millions; 1961: 50·6 millions), by reason of the enlargement of the territory and of natural growth. The birthrate has a tendency to fall (from 32% in 1911 to 20% in 1964) but as mortality decreases too, the annual increase remains the same, 11% in both 1861 and 1961. The population would be much larger if, between 1861 and 1963, 27 million Italians had not left their country in search of work. Six millions returned home, while 21 millions settled permanently abroad. It will also be noted that:

(1) There is an internal population movement from the south to the north (and particularly to the Genoa–Turin–Milan triangle).
(2) There is a rural exodus.
(3) The population's average age is rising (from 28·5 years in 1911 to 33·6 years in 1961).

IV. THE ITALIAN ECONOMY

Agriculture retains its importance (29% of the active population). Emphasis must be laid on the high percentage of cultivated land (51%) as against the areas taken up by forest (18%) and by meadows and pastures (17%). But these percentages differ appreciably from one area to another. Thus while in the Venetian Po valley area and in many of the plains and uplands of central Italy the climate and soil permit rational and mechanized agriculture and the cultivation of highly profitable products (rice, hemp, sugar beet), southern Italy is devoted to extensive agriculture (with the exception of the Campania plain, the Conca d'Oro of Palermo, certain irrigated areas of Apulia, etc.).

Climate, nature of holding, and soil permit a great variety of types of cultivation (predominance of mixed agriculture). There is nevertheless a difference between continental Italy, which is more suitable for annual grain cultivation (wheat, maize, rice), and peninsular Italy, where the conditions are more favourable for Mediterranean cultivation (vine, olives, figs, fruit trees, and, where irrigation is possible, citrus fruit and vegetables, which contest with the very widespread extensive cereal growing of Sicily and Apulia).

Stockbreeding is a traditional Italian occupation, and here, too, the contrast between continental and peninsular Italy is very marked. In the Venetian lower Po plains, climate and soil permit permanent cultivation of fields and the growing of forage crops such as clover and lucerne. These meadows are used for the raising of cattle, which provide milk, butter, and meat. Cattle-breeding is often combined with arable farming and there are many mixed farms. In central and southern Italy, on the other hand, the long summer droughts and rough ground permit only grazing, and the uncultivated land is left to sheep and goats. Moreover, an economy based on sheep-breeding is usually independent of arable farming.

In the matter of mineral resources Italy has not been favoured by nature. Recently modest quantities of petroleum have been discovered in Emilia, the Abruzzi, and Sicily: the annual production amounts to some 2·7 million tons. However, although Italy lacks petrol, it has numerous refineries which in 1964 treated 57·5 million tons of crude oil. A pipeline links Genoa with Switzerland and Germany. On the other hand, Italy is fairly rich in natural gas (deposits in the Lodi and Cortemaggiore area, the Po and Polesine delta, Lucania, etc.). In southern Tuscany, there are geothermic resources.

In Italy 41 % of the active population work in industry, so that the country has acquired an agricultural-industrial physiognomy.

The conditions favouring industry are:

(1) An abundance of agricultural raw materials requiring processing (wheat, fruit for bottling, tomatoes, etc.).
(2) The availability of an abundant, intelligent, and capable labour force.
(3) Abundant electric power resources.

Italy now produces huge quantities of steel (1964: 9·8 million tons), and its metallurgical and machine industry is able to manufacture large numbers of motor-cars, typewriters, sewing machines, etc. Considerable progress has also been achieved in the field of cellulose and synthetic fibres, fertilizers, cement, etc.

Even in the distribution of industry the contrast between north and south is very marked: two-thirds of all workers are to be found in northern Italy—Lombardy, Piedmont, Liguria, Venice, Trieste, Ferrara region.

In the assessment of Italy's foreign trade the following three factors should be borne in mind:

(1) The opening of the big Alpine tunnels (rail and road) which facilitate relations with the Transalpine countries.

(2) The piercing of the Isthmus of Suez, which reopened the eastern trade routes.

(3) The fact that Italy, extending across the middle of the Mediterranean and joined to Europe by the Po plain, is of major importance as a transit country. Communications have recently been improved by the development of the motorway network whose principal axis is the Autostrada del Sole.

Italy imports fuel, industrial raw materials, and food-stuffs (cereals, meat, fish, coffee, etc.). It exports agricultural products, including citrus and other fruits, vegetables, and industrial products such as textiles, machinery, or chemical products.

ELIO MIGLIORINI
Professor of Geography
University of Rome

LUXEMBOURG

The Grand Duchy of Luxembourg dates from the Treaty of Vienna in 1815; its present frontiers are the result of the Belgian revolution and were fixed by the Treaty of London (1839).

Geology and Morphology

In spite of its small area (2586 sq. km.), Luxembourg is very varied in landscape.

In the north the Oesling (32 % of the area of the country) forms part, with the Ardennes, of the schistous Rhineland Massif, and consists of Devonian strata, mainly schists. It is an ancient massif in the form of a horizontal peneplain at an average height of 450 m., which has undergone rejuvenation, as can be seen in the incised valleys. The hillsides are covered with spruce and thickets of oak mixed with broom. The plateau, whose soil lacks lime, supports intensive cereal and potato farming, thanks to the Thomas slag provided by the steelworks.

In the south the Gutland (Good-land) forms 68 % of the area of the country, at an average altitude of 350 m. It is composed of Triassic and Jurassic sedimentary strata in parallel strips between the Oesling and the Hunsrück, ending north and east in sandstone and limestone cuestas. Various typical landscapes are found: the edge of the Oesling, a wide depression; the sandstone plateau of Luxembourg with large beech and oak forests, and fields on the sandy plateau; the slopes of the Moselle valley, covered by vineyards that produce a dry, light wine; the south-west with its iron-ore deposits which explain the remarkable industrial development.

Population

The total population of 335,000 includes 17 % foreigners, concentrated mainly in the southern steel-working region.

The density is 129 per sq. km. Luxembourg, the capital, has a population of 77,000, and Esch-sur-Alzette, the steel centre, 28,000.

The birth-rate (14·8‰) and the death-rate (12·3‰) leave a surplus of births of only 2·5‰, and this is definitely on the downward trend.

The living standard is very high.

Language

In the Grand Duchy a Moselle dialect is spoken, but French and German are the official languages.

The position of the country between Belgium, France, and Germany, between the Moselle and Meuse basins, and its bilingualism, account for its role as a European forum (Luxembourg was the original seat of the European Coal and Steel Community (ECSC).

Economy

Industry employs 45% of the working population.

The basic industry is steel, dominated by the ARBED–HADIR trust, which produces 4·5 million tons of steel annually, including 3·5 million tons of sheet metal products, the highest per capita production in the world.

Several medium-sized processing industries have developed considerably, mainly for export: they include metal-construction work and pottery and the manufacture of tiles and tobacco.

Many new industries, mostly foreign (39 after the Second World War) are beginning to make a breach in the monolithic Luxembourg economy; among the most important plants are the Goodyear tyre factory and the Dupont de Nemours and Monsanto plastics factories.

We must finally add the tourist industry, with 700,000 overnight stays of foreigners in hotels and boarding-houses.

Electric power is provided from the thermal power-stations in the steel region, but the country has made great progress in developing hydro-electric power—the dam at Esch-sur-Sûre, the dam at Rosport, and the hydro-electric power-station fed by pumped storage at Vianden.

Agriculture, which employs 13% of the working population, is highly mechanized and intensive, but suffers from the dividing up of the land into small plots, little progress being made with redistribution. Small and medium-sized holdings definitely predominate (54% under 30 ha.). Out of the 1355 sq. km. of productive land, 49% is arable, producing cereals (wheat, rye, barley, oats), mangelwurzels, and potatoes, and 49·5% is meadowland and pasture, supporting a stock of 183,000 cattle. When 116,000 pigs are also taken into consideration we realize that farming is now shifting towards stock-breeding.

Transport and Trade

Transport by road, by rail (mainly electrified), by the canalized Moselle (port of Mertert), and by direct airlines to Brussels, Paris,

Frankfurt, London, and New York gives the country a strong position as an international cross-roads.

Luxembourg is a member of the Belgian–Luxembourg Economic Union, Benelux, and the European Economic Community. 66·5% of its exports are to countries belonging to the Community, and 33·5% to other countries. For steel alone, exports account for 93·8% of total production.

JOSEPH POEKER
Professor àé Athenée Grand Ducal
Luxembourg

MALTA

The Maltese Islands are a compact group of limestone outcrops. Their total land area is only 122 sq. miles, the largest island, Malta itself, being some fifteen miles long and seven wide. Their position in the middle of the 'inland sea', together with a fine natural harbour, has given the country an importance out of all proportion to its size. Since the beginning of historic times the Maltese Islands have been successively dominated by the Phoenicians, the Carthaginians, the Romans, the Arabs, the Normans, the Aragonese, the Castilians, the Knights of St John, the French, and the British. Round the harbour and the old capital of Mdina there are numerous defensive works. Malta has been well named the Island Fortress of the Mediterranean.

This small country is not solely a strategic fortress. Behind the harbour and the ever-expanding urban area surrounding it stretches a distinctive rural landscape arising from a unique combination of physical, social, and demographic circumstances. The two associated landscapes compete for the very limited land resources of the island. Until recently the population was concentrated immediately round the harbour and to a much lesser extent in a number of villages spread over the island. This pattern is now fast changing. The urban area is increasing round the harbour, absorbing a number of neighbouring villages. Farther afield ribbon development is joining together villages which once formed compact, well-defined units.

Rural Landscape

Away from this urban area compact villages of flat-roofed houses (reminiscent of Southern Europe and of North Africa) are regularly scattered over the countryside. These villages are tightly enclosed in a dense matrix of small, irregular fields divided by dry limestone walls. *Morcellement*, or land sub-division, is in an advanced state here. When the ground starts to slope the plots are terraced to prevent erosion. While the rainfall of Malta averages only 20½ in., autumn rainstorms may break suddenly after months of drought, causing havoc on the terraces of light soils. On the plateaux, which rise to levels of 400 and 800 ft, much of the land is bare karst, but even here farmers have laboriously collected soil from pockets in the rock, and created small walled fields. Simple wind-pumps, standing up above the maze of walls, haul up water from a clay layer below the limestone. Everywhere the use of land is intensive. Where building-stone has been quarried the original surface soil is replaced and cultivation continued surrounded by a rock-face. When building is proposed on agricultural land, soil must by law be stripped off and cultivated in fields elsewhere. This led one author to conclude that "in the last analysis, it is not the actual physical conditions which control man's activities—it is the view that man himself takes of what can or cannot be done which really matters."

Urban Economy

Although much of the landscape is agricultural, the economy of the country is not an agricultural one. Farming accounted for only 6·4% of the Gross National Product in 1964. Recent advances have been made in poultry breeding and horticulture, but the limitations of the environment give little scope for any substantial increases in the total agricultural contribution.

More significant in this respect are the Dockyard, manufacturing industry, and tourism, all sectors of the economy receiving special attention in the five-year plans inaugurated in 1959. The purpose of these plans is to create new exports to offset the withdrawal of the British Forces. Recent developments in the harbour area have been rapid and striking. Since the British finally abandoned the naval base in 1959–60, conversion to a commercial ship-repair yard has been going ahead. Several docks have been enlarged to take modern tankers, and workshops have been modernized. Unemployment caused by the withdrawal of the British Navy is still considerable, but the position is expected to improve. (13,036 people worked in the Dockyard in March 1958, only 5244 in March 1966.)

Close to the harbour are three industrial estates. These, and new industry elsewhere, are an important part of the programme to diversify the economy. Most new establishments receive the Government aid offered to industry attracting employment and contributing to exports. As a result, production and employment are improving: in 1965, commercial production reached £4·75 millions, more than three-quarters being sold abroad. Employment in aided industries rose from 680 in 1962 to more than 2800 in 1965.

Advertisement and the development of hotels have helped to attract increasing numbers of tourists. In 1965 tourists spent £2·5 millions, and in 1968–69 they are expected to bring in £6·6 millions.

I

Until recently Malta's Mediterranean climate and beautiful coastline have attracted surprisingly few visitors.

In spite of these hopeful trends Malta's total exports still amount to only £10·75 millions, a small figure compared with her imports of £38·88 millions (1966).

Population Problem

Malta is exceptional among European countries in having retained her nuptial fertility at the level of the late nineteenth century, although recently there have been signs of smaller families. The country now has the highest average family size (about 3·5 children) and average density of population (3075 per sq. mile) of any country in Europe. It is hardly surprising that there is emigration. Maltese have been leaving their country in large numbers (61,000 between 1950 and 1961), most for Australia, the United Kingdom, Canada, and the USA.

The pressure of numbers on meagre natural resources has given rise over the centuries to today's remarkable rural scene of intensive cultivation and the hardiness and ingenuity of the farmers. Until now the pressure has always been relieved by the external wealth of occupying Powers who valued the country for its strategic harbour. With modern developments in weaponry and long-range shipping this asset has declined in value. The harbour, the country's greatest physical resource, must now be completely modernized to compete with the great commercial ports of Europe, and with this the multitudes in the towns around the harbour will need to adapt themselves to new types of work. The Maltese are now trying to overcome the consequences of a too narrowly based economy. Migration is bound to continue, but with an increasingly viable economy Malta may hope to become a genuinely independent and prosperous nation.

K. W. BRUCE, B.A., M. PHIL.
Oxford Research Student

THE NETHERLANDS

Among the most remarkable geographical characteristics of the Netherlands is the combination of its very high population density (370 per sq. km.) and the fact that some 50 % of the country (south-west, west, north-west, and the central river belt) is below average high-tide level (deepest point 6·6 m.). Moreover, almost 50 % of the total population lives and works in the central-western part of the country (20 % of the total area). This part is highly industrialized and has many cities—there are sixteen with populations of over 50,000, of which three are over half a million (Amsterdam, Rotterdam, The Hague[1]). The overcrowding in this city area, called the *Randstad* (4 million people), results in housing, traffic, and recreational difficulties, and is connected with several other problems. Since most of the area is below sea-level and the ground is not firm, land prices, building costs, road construction costs, and rents are as a rule considerably higher than in other parts of the country. This and other low-lying parts of the country are protected against flooding by river and sea dikes, and, along the North Sea coast, by the dunes.

The Netherlands has:

(*a*) The highest birth-rate in Western Europe—19·9‰ (higher in the southern, Roman Catholic part, Brabant and Limburg; lower in the western and northern Protestant parts).

(*b*) The lowest death-rate in Europe (7·9 %).

(*c*) An infant death-rate (under 1 year) which is the world's second lowest (14·4‰ babies, after Sweden with 14·2).

This gives it the world record in population density. Although the birth-rate has been falling since 1875, the death-rate has fallen faster, resulting in an increasing population growth—5·1 million in 1900, 7·9 million in 1930, 12·5 million in 1966.

From this situation—a rapidly growing population in a very small (33,860 sq. km.; including water 36,100 sq. km.) and already

---

[1] 1966—862,000 (conurbation 950,000); 728,000 (conurbation 1,050,000); and 593,000 (conurbation 730,000) respectively, the first being the capital, the second the world's biggest port, and the third the seat of the national government.

crowded country—the question arises: how does the Netherlands succeed in feeding its population and providing employment for the growing numbers? When more data are taken into account the question becomes yet more pressing:

(a) Really rich soils are limited, which means that only a rather small percentage of the nation's soils can be used for growing commercial crops such as wheat, sugar beet, flax. The climate restricts the growing of the more valuable fruits and vegetables (grapes, peaches, tomatoes, etc.) to expensive hothouse production.

(b) Natural resources are also limited, so that raw materials for industry have largely to be imported. There are salt, coal, some oil, no metal ores, little wood. In 1961 a huge reserve of natural gas was discovered in the province of Groningen, near the village of Slochteren (known reserve at least 1900 billion cub. m. which is being exploited now as a source of low-cost energy, both for industrial and domestic use, and as a cheap raw material for the chemical industry. Moreover, increasing quantities are being exported annually. However, in combination with the effects of the international coal crises, this new resource completely ruined Dutch coalmining and coke production (anthracite—Kerkrade, Brunssum, etc.; bituminous coal, coke, and chemical works—Geleen, etc.). Several mines have been closed, including one of the safest and most modern in Europe, with some 8000 workers (near Geleen, in 1969). The schedule of closing means that before 1977 new employment has to be created for some 40,000 people, including population growth; consequently an extensive Government programme for industrial reorientation of the mining region was set up and has been working successfully since 1966.

The distribution of soils is a factor in the economic situation. The part of the country lying above average sea-level (roughly the eastern part) is covered by either poor or rather difficult soils. These are Pleistocene sands (partly in Saale, pushed in front of the ice-sheet, now wood-covered ridges—Veluwe and North Twenthe); and mostly low-lying, partly stripped Holocene peat soils and alluvial clay soils, which must be drained in order to improve their ground-water situation. Only the southernmost part of Limburg (highest point of the Netherlands is Vaals, 321 m.), which, as the northern edge of the (Belgian) Ardennes peneplain, is an uplifted intersected plateau, has rich loess soils (post Saale).

The generally mixed farming pattern of the east and south (higher sections forested) has different regional specializations (various patterns of dairying, pig and chicken breeding, horticulture) depending on such things as market situation, ground-water level, soil quality. A remarkable exception to this pattern is on the completely man-made soil of the East Groningen–Drenthe area, a former moor where the underlying glacial sands were made into good agricultural soil (seventeenth to nineteenth century) by mixing with the carefully kept topsoil of the original peat landscape, and with compost made out of garbage. Heavily fertilized, this man-made soil is still good cropland (potatoes, rye, even sugar beet and wheat).

Behind the dunes and dikes the low-lying, Holocene south-west, west, and upper northern parts of the country consist partly of marine clays, partly of peat soils, both of which generally have to be pumped and drained artificially. This means that almost all the country constantly requires a high rate of expenditure on drainage and/or fertilizers, to make and keep the soils usable. To an extreme extent this is the case in the low parts of the Netherlands. Here there is a series of *polders*, each polder being a piece of land, small or large, surrounded by dikes and intersected for drainage by a system of canals through which the water-level is regulated. The surplus water (precipitation), unable to flow away by gravity since the polder surface is below the water-level outside the dikes, has to be pumped out into a ring canal surrounding the dike, or into a stream or lake, all of higher water-level than the polder. From there the water is conducted to a river or canal, either by means of sluices or again by pumping. The river or canal is either open to the sea or closed by big sluices. In some cases, where at low tide the sea or open river falls below the polder water-level, (high polders), or groups of polders together, drain into the sea or river directly through sluices, without pumping.

Most polders are organized in groups, the *Waterschappen* (water authorities), each of which forms a unit within a bigger dike surrounding the total *waterschap* and has a central system of draining. The canals, lakes, and small rivers in between the dikes of the separate polders of the *waterschap* hav ebeen included in the bigger system now and serve as an important provisional reservoir to store water that cannot be drained away immediately and to supply water to the various polders in dry summers. This may account for the existence of rather a number of lakes and seemingly useless canals in a country reclaiming new land from the sea, a contradiction often puzzling both to foreigners and natives.

These waters are highly necessary as provisional storage for surplus water. The lakes and bigger canals are also important recreation areas. Nowadays almost all pumping (for centuries the work of windmills) is done by electric or diesel engines. Hundreds of windmills have disappeared, others are falling into decay, a few are restored for their beauty and the tourists. Not all polders are similar. Some polders are diked and drained swampy peatlands (in South and North Holland and West Utrecht) kept in grass (peat requires a high ground-water level), with eventually some horti-culture. Others were reclaimed from the sea (in the north of Groningen and Friesland, almost the total south-west archipelago, and the twentieth-century IJsselmeerpolders) or from former lakes. Both have clay soils, but their land use depends on ground-water level, soil structure, allotment pattern, situation, tradition, etc.

Although various agricultural regions are basic to the national economy because they supply high-value export products[1], and although agricultural export makes up some 25 % of the total export, agriculture is only a minor and decreasing activity in the Netherlands, (less than 9 % of the working population). To a great extent based on geographical site and situation, services at home and abroad (over 47 % of the working population) and manufacturing (over 42 %) are much more important, and this explains the very dense population and the relatively high standard of living. Holland is in the heart of Western Europe, bounded by the North Sea, the world's busiest sea route, and on the mouth of Europe's commercially most impor-tant river, the Rhine. It has a favourable position between leading manufacturing and sea-faring countries.

Of the two big ports of the Netherlands, Rotterdam enjoys an

---

[1] Dairying, wheat, flax, and especially flowers and plants from, for instance, the hothouses in the Aalsmeer peat region south-west of Amster-dam; flower-bulbs from the dug-off dunes along the North Sea coast, mainly between Leiden and Haarlem; and vegetables, tomatoes, and other soft fruits from the hothouses on the man-made soils of the Westland south of The Hague.

open connection with the North Sea (via the c. 24-km.-long canal at the mouth of the Rhine, the New Waterway), whereas ships to Amsterdam have to pass huge sea locks in the c. 22-km.-long North Sea Canal.

Both are depôts and entrepôts as well as transit ports, although Rotterdam (because of its open connection with Germany and Switzerland for ships of up to 2000 tons) is more of a transit port (oil, cereals, ores) than Amsterdam, for the Amsterdam–Rhine Canal (also up to 2000 tons) has some locks. The booming growth of the port areas is absorbing considerable space west of the towns. The Rotterdam area already occupies the whole distance to the sea, with new basins, refineries (pipelines to the German Ruhr), yards, and manufacturing areas. Even farther west the complex called *Europoort* (Gate of Europe) is still partly under construction and includes port basins in the sand-banks off the coast for quick dispatch of tomorrow's mammoth tankers and ore carriers.

Small wonder that today the ports of Rotterdam and Amsterdam proper are just a part of two complex manufacturing regions at the mouths of the Rhine and IJssel respectively, forming the south and the north wing of the Randstad and including a number of smaller ports and manufacturing towns. Several of them belong to once independent manufacturing areas (Dordrecht—shipbuilding, metal; IJmuiden/Velsen—fish, steelmaking, paper; Zaanregion—foodstuffs, woodworking) and are based partly on modern port activities and deep-water location, partly on historical functions. Manufacturing in other parts of the country sometimes clearly dominates an area, or else is only a part of a more varied occupational pattern. Often, however, owing to intensive commuting, manufacturing is easily the main source of work and income (northern peatmoors, Twenthe, eastern and central Brabant, South Limburg). In very general terms, the official 129 economic geographical units of the Netherlands could be compressed to an elementary pattern, from north to south:

1. The marine clay arable and mixed farming area (North Groningen, the IJsselmeerpolders, some western lake polders and the south-west archipelago.

2. The north-east peatmoor manufacturing and arable region (East Groningen–Drenthe: potato flour, strawboard, chemicals, light metal, nylon, and nylon wear).

3. The Pleistocene sands mixed farming area (grass predominating) with scattered industries and leisure areas (Drenthe, Overijssel, Gelderland, North Limburg).

4. The northern and western dairy regions (Friesland, North and South Holland, West Utrecht).

5. The Eastern textile/metal manufacturing area (South Twenthe— Enschede, Hengelo, Almelo, Oldenzaal).

6. The western manufacturing and commercial area (Randstad) apart from Rhine and IJmouth:

> (a) The Utrecht–Hilversum–Amersfoort triangle (manufacturing as well as residential and leisure area, with Utrecht an important traffic and (inter)national meeting centre.
> (b) The Hague, mainly administrative and residential.
> (c) The towns of Delft and Leiden with varied functions.

7. The South and East Veluwe manufacturing, residential, and recreation areas (centres—Arnhem, Apeldoorn).

8. The central river clay, dairy, and fruit-growing region.

9. The central and eastern Brabant manufacturing/mixed farming region, Breda (varied), Tilburg (woollens), Eindhoven (Philips radio, T.V., and varied electronics, DAF cars), Oss (meat-packing, chemicals, carpets); with Randstad, by far the most important economic region of the Netherlands.

10. The South Limburg (declining) mining, manufacturing, and recreation area (see above).

11. Scattered horticultural regions (Westland—tomatoes; the dune bulb region—Boskoop, Aalsmeer, Venlo).

Apart from already mentioned problems (Randstad; mining) the outstanding human geographical problems of the country concern:

1. The defence against the sea. Since the 1953 disaster, when many dikes in the south-west were burst, the Delta Plan has been in execution with the purpose of:

> (a) A better defence against the (rising) sea by closing the estuaries, except the Wester Schelde, which is the entrance to Antwerp (Belgium).
> (b) Creating freshwater reservoirs
>> (i) To fight the increasing salination of agricultural soils.
>> (ii) For drinking water.
>> (iii) For recreation.

(c) The opening of the isolated province of Zeeland by a bridge (Zeelandbrug) between the islands of Noord Beveland and Schouwen, 5022 m.).

2. Regional industrialization. Owing to decreasing agricultural employment and to structural difficulties (textiles, coal-mining), industry or more varied industry is necessary in some northern, eastern, and southern regions. Moreover, a spatial redistribution of employment is needed to relieve crowded Randstad and to help north, east, and south.

3. The need for recreation areas. Owing to the increasing population, careful planning for recreation is necessary. The traditional recreation areas (Veluwe, South Limburg, East Gelderland, the lake districts of South Holland and Friesland, the North Sea beach and the Wadden islands) being short of space and facilities, new areas are under development—e.g., along the IJsselmeer and delta area coasts.

W. W. DE JONG
Lecturer
Groningen University

NORWAY

Norway is one of the European countries where the relationship between geological and climatic conditions on the one hand and settlement and industries on the other is most obvious.

The Norwegian bedrock is very old. Except for the territories of Spitzbergen and Jan Mayen, there are practically no geological formations in Norway younger than the Paleozoic. Large areas in the eastern part of the country and also elsewhere—*e.g.*, in the county of Finnmark—are Pre-Cambrian mountains. Sedimentary rocks originating from layers of clay and limestone dating from the Cambro-Silurian age are found, for instance, in the flat country in the east, around the lake of *Mjøsa*, the largest in Norway. The so-called Silurian counties in the east are among the most fertile agricultural districts in Norway.

The Caledonian mountain folding is apparent in the landscape. A number of fjords along the western coast are in the general direction south-west to north-east (*cf.* similar formations in Scotland). Coastal steamers largely follow these fjords. Some of the valleys, especially those in the county of Nordland, run in the same general direction. The railway and the main road in Nordland follow some of these valleys.

In the Tertiary period the land in Western Norway rose considerably, and the wild landscape of the fjord district was then largely transformed to its present shape. (Glittertind, 2472 m., Sognefjord, the longest fjord, 183 km.)

The present distribution of soil is a result of what took place during and after the last Ice Age. Up to about 10,000 years ago Norway as well as Sweden was covered by a thick and heavy layer of ice. Towards the end of this period the land had sunk, and after the retreat of the ice the sea covered large areas of what is dry land today. In the Oslo area the sea-level was about 220 m. higher than it is now.

Today we find much fertile soil on this former sea-bed. This type of landscape is exposed to erosion by running water. We therefore find many small valleys carved out by streams in the clay-land below the former sea-level. All things considered, this soil is among the most fertile in Norway.

In the western part of the country we sometimes find similar beds along the innermost parts of the longest fjords, but here only a very small area was covered by sea at the end of the last Ice Age. At the end of the last glacial period the sea-level in these parts of the country was only a few feet above the present level. Even so we find that most of the population in western Norway has settled on a low and comparatively flat fringe of land along the sea, known as the coastal plain.

Climate and Flora

Parts of Norway lie between the same latitudes as parts of Greenland and northern Siberia, but climatic conditions in Norway are much more favourable. Winds and sea currents generally come from the south-west, bringing mild air and comparatively warm sea water towards the coast. With some simplification one may say that the mild climate is caused by the North Atlantic Drift. The whole western coast benefits from the mild sea currents during winter: the average temperature at the North Cape (71°N.) is no lower than that of the Po Basin in January—*i.e.*, about 0°C. Ice-breakers are not needed in the fjords of western and northern Norway.

In eastern Norway the climate is more continental. The average temperature for January in Oslo is about −4°C., for July about17°C. The inland areas in the east and the Finnmark Plateau have severe winters with an average temperature as low as −15°C. in January.

The country has a high precipitation, but it is unequally distributed. Some mountain areas have an annual precipitation of more than 3 m., whereas the upper part of the Gudbrandsdalen Valley (Lesja, Skjak, and Lom) has practically none at all. The Finnmark Plateau has also very little precipitation.

In the cool climate the level of evaporation is low and the amount of water reaching the rivers is therefore considerable. The mountain plateaux with many swamps and lakes (and glaciers) serve as natural reservoirs and to some extent even out the amount of water. Extensive dams and water tunnels have also been constructed. These secure a comparatively even supply of water to the many large hydro-electric plants which today constitute one of the most important resources of the country.

Thanks to the precipitation there is a comparatively rich vegetation of grass and bushes both along the coast and in the mountains. Along the southern coast a few deciduous trees are found—*e.g.*, oak —but the large forests in eastern and central Norway consist of evergreens, pine, and spruce. North of the Arctic Circle pines grow in the valleys. In the mountains and in North Norway wide areas are covered by mountain birch.

It is estimated that about one-quarter of the total area of Norway is covered by productive forests. Only about 3% of the country is cultivated land. But the mountain plateaux and other areas usually counted as unproductive serve as pastures for domestic animals.

The population of Norway was about 3·8 million in 1966. The area is 324,000 sq. km. (Spitzbergen excluded). This gives an average of 12 persons per sq. km. But the population is not evenly distributed over the country. The large mountain plateaux are too high to have any permanent population.

Industries

The industries of Norway are developed on the basis of the country's natural resources, above all the arable land, the forests, the water-power, and the sea (fisheries and navigation).

Modern agriculture is, in Norway as in other countries, more specialized than in the past. Grain production is now practically limited to the lowlands and almost exclusively used for feeding domestic animals. Grain for consumption by human beings is imported. The most important among Norwegian agricultural products are milk, meat, and fur (especially from mink). There are more sheep in Norway than in all the other Nordic countries put together. Along the coast the sheep may graze outside during most of the winter. Reindeer raising is of some importance, especially in north Norway. The reindeer feed on the pastures along the coast in summer and inland during the winter.

The inner parts of the western fjord district have large crops of fruit. Considerable amounts of sweet cherries, apples, and other kinds of fruit are sent from here to other parts of the country.

The Norwegian forests provide raw materials for a very important pulp and paper industry. Most of this industry is located on either side of the Oslo fjord and along the coast as far south as Kristiansand; but the pulp and paper industry is also found in Trøndelag, in central Norway.

The types of industry which are most dependent upon hydro-electric power are largely found along the fjords in western and northern Norway. Most of the *chemical industry* owned by Hydro is found in the county of Telemark. The large Norwegian aluminium industry is growing rapidly. Bauxite (and alumina) for this production are imported. Apart from this, there are some other electro-metallurgical factories dependent on hydro-electric power.

An important shipbuilding industry is found in towns along the coast, especially in southern Norway.

The modern food-production industry has created a new situation for the Norwegian fishing industry. The herring and cod fisheries are the most important. Best known is the seasonal fishing of large cod which takes place in winter off the Lofoten Islands. This has undergone great changes during the last few years: in 1966 only about 5000 fishermen took an active part in it; some years ago there were five or six times as many.

The country still has a considerable export market for dried fish and *klippfish* (salted and dried codfish), although a large number of factories for frozen-fish products have been built since the Second World War. Frozen fish fillets are now close to being the most important product of Norwegian fisheries. This is particularly important to the county of Finnmark, where people are more dependent on fishing than anywhere else in the country and where the export of fresh fish to large foreign markets used to be virtually impossible because of the long transport routes.

The large catches of herring are primarily used in the oil industry. Oil is also produced from whales. Norway has been the leading nation in whaling both in the Arctic and the Antarctic, with a large number of 'floating factories' in Antarctic waters. But the number of whales is dwindling, and so is the profit. It is doubtful if Norwegians will carry on whaling in the Antarctic in the future.

But the nation's most important source of income is the modern commercial fleet, which is one of the largest in the world. Only Great Britain has a commercial fleet substantially larger than that of Norway. During the post-war period the Norwegian commercial fleet has been among the world's four largest, sometimes the second (in terms of active tonnage).

Norway is a kingdom. The king resides in the capital, Oslo. Here are also the National Assembly and the Government.

It is convenient to divide the country into five parts: East Norway, South Norway, West Norway, Central Norway, and North Norway.

Important towns outside Oslo are Drammen and Fredrikstad in East Norway, Kristiansand in South Norway, Stavanger and Bergen in West Norway, Trondheim in Central Norway, and Tromsø in North Norway. Hammerfest is generally referred to as the most northerly town in the world.

The longest river is the Glomma (611 km.). The highest mountain is the Glittertind (2472 m. above sea-level, including the glacier at the top). The Galhøpiggen is 2469 m.

The longest fjord is Sognefjord (183 km.).

Norway offers great possibilities for camping, skiing, and hiking. Skiing is a sport practised by almost everybody. The best-known skiing event is the Holmenkollen competitions which take place near Oslo around the 1st March each year. Norway has two official languages, but they are so alike that people who speak the different forms of Norwegian easily understand each other. Most of the Lapp population in the north are Norwegians, but there are also Lapps in Sweden and Finland (and a few in the Soviet Union). The Norwegian Lapps are taught both their own language and Nowegian at school.

DR ØIVIND RØDEVAND
Lecturer, Ullern High School
Oslo

PORTUGAL

I. PHYSICAL GEOGRAPHY

(1) *Geographical Position and Area*

Situated in south-western Europe on the Iberian Peninsula between Spain and the Atlantic, Portugal, a stretch of land measuring 89,619 sq. km., is closely bound up with the sea. The adjacent archipelagos of Madeira (783 sq. km.) and of the Azores (2304 sq. km.) are the insular extension of Portugal.

(2) *Geology and Geomorphology*

Geologically, most of the territory is Iberian *Meseta*, an ancient, Primary rock formation where granite, schist, and gneiss predominate. In the west the coastal land from Espinho to the Tagus basin is of more recent, Secondary and Tertiary formation, comprising sandstone, clay, and limestone, often divided up by ridges bearing several lines of karst erosion (Estremenho limestone mountain mass). The low, flat south coast of Algarve, too, is of Secondary and Tertiary formation. The plain surrounding the mouths of the Tagus and Sado rivers is composed of more recent (Tertiary and Quaternary) fluvial and marine sedimentation.

The Iberian Meseta is divided in two by a central mountain range running from north-east to south-west, consisting, in Portugal, of a mountain chain commanded by the range of the Estrela (the Star, 1991 m.), which is merely a large *horst* bearing traces of Quaternary glaciation. This mountain range, stretching from the frontier to Lusia, divides Portugal into two parts which differ markedly from every point of view. Portugal is indeed a country of contrasts—contrasts between north and south, between coastal area and interior.

The region north of the Tagus is largely mountainous. The mountains are generally situated obliquely in relation to the coastline and afford easy access to the humid Atlantic winds which penetrate far into the interior. The coast north of the Tagus thus has a more abundant rainfall, lusher vegetation, is more suitable for agriculture, and is more densely populated. The interior of continental Portugal consists mainly of plateaux and deeply entrenched rivers. With its sparser rainfall and severe winters, it is less suitable for agriculture and less densely populated.

The countryside south of the Tagus is different, consisting of many broad plains including the Tertiary plains of the Tagus and Sado rivers and the impoverished peneplain of Alentejo with its residual hills, bounded in the south by the Algarve mountains. These form an amphitheatre slanting southward towards the sea. The area has a dry Mediterranean climate with scant rainfall and very hot summers; it is sparsely populated except for the Algarve coastal area.

Because of the general south-western slant of the Iberian Meseta, all the Peninsula's big rivers (Douro, Tagus, Guadiana) flow across Portugal into the Atlantic. They are unfitted for navigation over most of their course, but have considerable hydro-electric potential. The Tagus alone has a broad estuary where the port of Lisbon has been established and developed.

(3) *Climate and Vegetation*

Situated in a zone of climatic transition where Atlantic and Mediterranean influences meet, Portugal does not have a uniform climate. The coastal belt north of the Tagus has a fairly temperate maritime climate: the heat remains moderate throughout the year, the rainfall is abundant, winters are mild, and summers not unduly hot. It is a region of deciduous oak, sea-pine, and meadows. In the interior the altitude and some continental influences from the Iberian Meseta produce severe winters and even snowfall. In this area we find deciduous oak and chestnut. The extensive area south of the Tagus is wholly different, having a Mediterranean climate which becomes more and more pronounced towards the south (Algarve coast). Throughout this area cork-oak and quercus ilex predominate, but the Algarve province is also known for its figs, almond, and carob trees. It may be said that the central part of Portugal, the Beiras, is an area of transition between coast and interior, between north and south, with moderate maritime, continental, or Mediterranean characteristics.

II. HUMAN GEOGRAPHY

Continental Portugal has a population of 8,700,000; with Madeira and the Azores it attains 9,000,000. The population density is high (over 100 per sq. km.). The population increases by 100,000 people a year. The population density is extremely high in the north-west (above all, around Oporto), in the Lisbon area, and on the Setubal Peninsula and the Algarve coast; it is low in the interior and the plains south of the Tagus.

Portugal is a country of emigrators. Its inhabitants, particularly those of the overpopulated north-west and the impoverished north-east, leave the country for Brazil, the Portuguese overseas territories, the United States, Venezuela, Argentina, Canada, France, Western Germany, and the Netherlands. Within the country itself many periodical migrations take place towards areas where at certain seasons the field work calls for additional labour.

Lately a relatively extensive movement of rural workers towards industry and services in urban centres (primarily Lisbon and Oporto) has also been recorded.

The population is predominantly rural. In the humid and wooded area north of the Tagus and in the Algarve region settlements are scattered; in the drier areas and open country south of the Tagus houses are grouped together.

The biggest towns are Lisbon and Oporto. Lisbon, the capital, situated on the right bank of the Tagus estuary, numbers 852,430 inhabitants (1 million with the surburban boroughs). The highly important port and long-standing tradition have made the town a major trade and shipping centre. The Lisbon international airport provides direct connections with all the main centres of Europe and America.

The biggest suspension bridge in Europe links Lisbon with the left bank of the Tagus, where another town is arising.

Oporto, with its 310,470 inhabitants (excluding the surburban population), is the country's second trade and industrial centre and virtually the economic (and cultural) capital of the whole northern part of the country.

The absence of major urban centres in the interior demonstrates Portugal's twofold character.

III. ECONOMIC GEOGRAPHY

(1) Agriculture, stockbreeding, forestry, and fishing account for 25% of the gross internal product (1965), but provide work for 40% of the total active population. A third of the land is untilled, the remainder being either very fertile or arable but of poor quality. Thanks to chemical fertilizers and mechanization, some areas have

already been reclaimed (primarily in the Alentejo and Ribatejo regions); however, traditional and archaic agricultural methods are still resorted to almost everywhere.

Forests cover a third of the land; the pines produce resin and the cork-oaks cork.

The eucalyptus tree provides not only timber but also wood-pulp and cellulose.

Cereal-growing is widespread, but the production is inadequate to cover consumption. Wheat is grown on the big farms south of the Tagus, almost always on a crop rotation/fallow-field system, the yield per hectare being very low. Maize is grown in the coastal area north of the Tagus, rye in the stony interior north of the same river. Rice is cultivated in the low and marshy basins of the Vouga, Mondego, Tagus, and Sado rivers. Vines, olives, potatoes, and fruit-trees are also cultivated, particularly the two former. The highly prized Portuguese wines (Basto, Amarante, Dao, Cartaxo, Colares, Setubal) include port, a major Portugese export.

Port is produced in the Alto Douro area between Barquinha and Barca d'Alva. The land in that area is schistous and summers are very hot. Three centuries ago the whole region was covered by evergreen oak. Man has transformed it into a country of vineyards planted on terraces resembling the steps of a gigantic staircase hewn into the rock; arable land has also been produced by ploughing some of the soils on the schist.

(2) In regard to stock breeding, the most important role in the Portuguese economy is played by pigs (Alentejo) and sheep and goats (Alentejo and the Beiras) as there are insufficient pastures to feed big herds of cattle.

(3) The fishing industry has always provided a livelihood for a large number of inhabitants (over 100,000). Tunny and sardine fishing form the basis of a highly progressive canning industry in the Algarve and Matosinhos areas. Portuguese fishermen also fish cod in the waters around Newfoundland and Greenland.

(4) Portugal lives primarily from the land and the sea, but development plans are directing the country's efforts towards industry. The rocks contain copper, tin, antimony, and iron, but ittle coal. Hydro-electric plants have therefore been built and have aided the setting-up of modern industries (chemical and pharmaceutical products, machines and electrical equipment, cellulose, rubber) and the development of old industries (spinning and weaving of wool, cotton, and horse-hair; cutlery, glassware and ceramics, paper).

The industrial sector employs 25 % of the active population and accounts for 42 % of the gross internal product; the figures for the services are, respectively, 37 % and 35 %.

(5) Portugal is a member of OECD and the European Free Trade Association.

MADEIRA

The archipelago of Madeira comprises the islands of Madeira and Porto Santo and some small uninhabited islands. It is situated south-west of Lisbon at a distance of some 340 sea-miles.

Madeira is a volcanic island of very uneven topography, with very high peaks and very deep valleys; the coastline consists of high and steep cliffs. The highest peak is the Pico Ruivo, which rises to 1861 m.

The island's southern side has a Mediterranean climate; the northern side is cooler and more humid.

The archipelago was uninhabited when it was discovered by Portuguese navigators in 1418. In 1960 Madeira and Porto Santo numbered 282,678 inhabitants—*i.e.*, 355 inhabitants per sq. km., hence mass emigration. The population lives primarily from rural activities and is spread over the coast in scattered settlements.

The mountain slopes had to be terraced, a whole network of irrigation dikes (*levadas*) built, and arable soil created. The agricultural production, tiered according to altitude, nature of soil, and climate, is distributed as follows:

(*a*) From sea-level up to 250 m., particularly in the southern part of the island, sugar-cane, bananas, and vines.

(*b*) From 250 m. to 750 m., wheat, maize, vines, and fruit-trees.

(*c*) From 750 m. to 1400 m., timber (pines and laurels) and scrub.

(*d*) Above 1400 m., grazing for sheep and goats. There are also many cows, but they are raised in the byre.

The main export is wine.

AZORES

The archipelago of the Azores is composed of nine islands spread over a length of some 500 sea-miles; it is situated west of the continent at a distance of some 850 miles.

The islands are of volcanic origin and volcanic activity continues (geysers, fumaroles, eruptions). The largest islands are São Miguel, Pico, and Terceira; the highest peak is in the island of Pico (2500 m.).

The Azores have a temperate, very humid, maritime climate with abundant rainfall.

The Azores were discovered by Portuguese navigators and were uninhabited. In 1960 the population numbered 336,933, with a density of 140 per sq. km. For a long time there has been massive emigration from these islands to the United States and Canada.

Agriculture is the main economic activity and includes the cultivation of cereals, potatoes, sweet potatoes, sugar beet, tobacco, tea, and pineapple (grown only in hothouses).

Administratively the archipelago is divided into three metropolitan 'districts' whose seats are the towns of Ponta Delgada (the natural port on the island of São Miguel), Angra do Heroismo (on the shore of the bay of the same name in the island of Terceira), and Horta (a port in the island of Faial).

Communication with the rest of the world is provided by the international airport of Santa Maria; there is a direct connection with New York. There are aerodromes on most of the islands and a Portuguese-American military airbase at Lajes (Terceira), which is also used to relieve the Santa Maria airport.

EVARISTO GUEDES VIEIRA
Professor of Geography Methodology
Lycée Normal of Pedro Nunes
Lisbon

SPAIN

The position of the Iberian Peninsula at the south-west corner of the European continent, solidly welded to it but also close to Africa, from which it is divided by fourteen km. of sea, and lying between the Mediterranean and the Atlantic, is an initial fact, full of geographical, physical, and human implications, which must be the starting-point for a study of the country. A junction for sea and land traffic as well as an Atlantic outpost, the peninsula has shared in all the adventures and experiences of the Mediterranean world. Neither the Pyrenees nor the Straits of Gibraltar in the south have constituted impassable boundaries. When the time came for the Spaniards and the Portuguese to explore the high seas the dormant Atlantic coast was transformed into a new sphere of activity where latent ocean-going talents became manifest.

The geographical relationship and affinity with the African continent apply only to North Africa, an integral part of the Mediterranean world, whose unity of physical and even human characteristics has only too frequently been overlooked by the traditional axiomatic division of the world into five. Moreover, North Africa was not, for the peoples of the peninsula, the infiltration route for African influences proper, or those from the south, but was the bridgehead for a process of orientalization which commenced in ancient times and reached its culmination with the arrival of the Arabs, although the irrigation system and other modifications of our geography sometimes attributed exclusively to them already had Roman precedents. What is taken for Africa in Spanish geography and culture should therefore be understood as Mediterranean, and, to a large extent, of oriental origin.

The most important feature of the peninsula's structure and relief is a large mass of elevated ground in the centre, the average height of which is between 600 and 800 m. The peninsula's mean altitude, double that of Europe in general but below that of Switzerland, is due more to this highland mass than to its mountains.

But this central mass, traditionally known in Spanish geography as the *Meseta* (Plateau), does not make up the whole of the Spanish hinterland. The Ebro Basin, despite its inland character, must not be included in it. Between the Meseta and the valley of the Ebro there is no structural continuity: if we go back to their earliest origins they appear as two distinct massifs, separated by a geosynclinal trough.

The insular shelf or palaeozoic substratum is found in the Ebro valley at a depth of 1500–2000 m., whereas it crops out to the west of the Meseta. Moreover, what is most important from the point of view of morphology and landscape, the Meseta is clearly distinguished by its higher altitude, by a mountain range, including the Iberian mountains, which separate it from the Ebro Basin, as well as by the conservation of a structural surface corresponding to the Tertiary sedimentation; because of greater erosive activity in the Ebro valley this is subject to a more pronounced process of drift, while in the Douro valley or northern half of the Meseta it emerges as a ring of flat, high tablelands and, in the southern area, in the region of La Mancha south of the Tagus Basin, it appears almost unbroken. But, in any case, the Meseta must not be presented to pupils in too simplified and schematic a form as a high plateau with a perfectly flat, even surface; it is, in fact, a raised agglomeration of land, composed of high, almost perfect horizontal surfaces (*paramos*), of eroded valleys and undulating plains, strewn with patches of ground situated lower than the high tablelands, but always above the plains which form the valley beds of the Ebro and the Guadalquivir.

In the interior of the Meseta one must again distinguish between the northern part (Old Castile and Leon) and the southern half (New Castile and Estremadura), separated by the central mountain system, including, among others and as its two main features, the Guadarrama and Gredos ranges. The northern part is higher than the southern (the average difference in altitude is 100 m.) and is more eroded; its boundaries coincide with those of the Douro Basin.

In addition to this north-south division, there is a structural division between west and east, clearly shown on the geological map. It is that which exists between the palaeozoic insular shelf outcropping in the west, composed of granite and other crystalline rocks, and reduced to a peneplain, and, in the east, a basin of mostly miocene sedimentary material (clay, marl, frequently gypseous, gravel, and, at a higher level though most has disappeared, lacustrine limestone). There is yet another difference distinguishing the northern from the southern half of the Meseta. In the north the old insular shelf extending westwards toward the ocean is only marginal, whereas in the south the shelf continued by the outcrop of the central system, which includes the Toledo mountains and the

Sierra Morena, is considerably developed; this marks the difference between the landscape of New Castile, whose most typical features correspond to the sedimentary basin, and the Estremadura peneplain. The latter's altitude, because of the Meseta's general swing to the west, falls below 400 m., and the Meseta is more easily accessible through the valley of the Tagus than on the rest of its perimeter.

Along the Meseta stretch two flat-bottomed sub-alpine rift valleys, bounded on the outside by the Pyrenees and the Baetic ranges. The Ebro valley is a triangular depression closed on all sides (Pyrenees, Iberian mountains, Catalan massif). The Guadalquivir valley or Baetican depression between the fold and part of the fault of the Sierra Morena, which forms the southern boundary of the Meseta and the Baetican mountains, is open to the Atlantic in the south-west.

To the north-west of the peninsula the Luso-Galician massif maintains a structural continuity with the western Meseta and with it makes up a large, ancient massif, the eastern part of which, broken and subsided, has remained fossilized by subsequent sedimentation (Mesozoic and Tertiary). But that structural continuity is no ground for including the north-west in the Meseta, for by its rougher and more complex relief faulted by an orthogonal system of fissures, by the existence of several impacted erosion surfaces peculiar to a rainy country, and especially by its oceanic climate and its vegetation, it constitutes a totally distinct geographical region.

Apart from the Meseta, with its structural extension to the north-west, the two valleys of the Ebro and the Guadalquivir and the Portuguese Mesozoic rim, the Cantabrian and Galician mountains to the north, and (with the exception of the south-west Baetics), the Catalan, Iberian, and Baetic ranges in the Levante and the south, all slope down to the sea. The coast is rectilinear without much indentation, except in the north-west (the Galician estuaries or *rias*), and there is no room for expansion of the coastal plains, whose fragmentary and feeble development is another characteristic of Spanish geography and one of the differences to be noted within the peninsula in relation to Portugal.

While recognizing the geographical individuality of the Meseta, an initial distinction may be made between the vast inner zone and the outer regions; but the similarity of climate, vegetation, and soil between the Ebro valley and the sedimentary portion of the Meseta also justifies a division between an inner or central and an outer or peripheral Spain. The latter may be subdivided into three main parts: firstly, Atlantic or Northern Spain, made up of the Basque country, the Asturias-Cantabrian region, and Galicia, which is clearly differentiated by its climatic conditions, vegetation, ethnology, agrarian structure, and economy; secondly, eastern Spain, where Catalonia must be distinguished from the Levante; finally, southern Spain or Andalusia, where a distinction must again be made between the Baetic plain, the mountains, and the coastal area.

Like France, Spain is a country of regional diversity. That point must be emphasized when teaching. Rather than variety, it would be more apt to speak of contrast, variety in France being more attenuated and gradual than in Spain. A diagonal line drawn from the north-west to the south-east, from Cape Finisterre to Cape Palos, would give the maximum range of contrasts offered by the geography of the peninsula.

At the last census (1960) the population in Spain numbered 30,430,398 inhabitants, equivalent to an average density of 60·2% per sq. km. Between 1857 (15,454,414 inhabitants) and 1950 (27,976,755 inhabitants) the increase was 81%. Between 1950 and 1960 the population increased by 2,453,943 inhabitants, 8·7% (an annual average rate of 0·87%).

During the same decade, out of 9200 Spanish municipalities, 6732 (75·3% of the total) registered a decrease in population. That applies particularly to those with the fewest inhabitants.

The birth-rate decreased from 33·6‰ in 1900 to 21·6‰ in 1960 (a higher figure than for 1950, when it was 20‰. Mortality went down from 28·3‰ in 1900 to 8·6‰ in 1960. The mean natural rate of increase during the decade was 1·14% per annum; the actual increase was 0·87%, the difference between the two figures being due to emigration (annual average 0·27%).

In all, between 1950 and 1960, 1,960,453 persons left their place of birth or usual residence, of whom 1,043,907 went to other parts of Spain and 916,545 went abroad.

The last decade has been marked by a migratory movement which has contributed seriously to depopulation of considerable areas of the Spanish countryside. The migrants go to the large towns and to foreign countries. The phenomenon of urban concentration has been considerably intensified during the last few years. In 1960 there were 24 towns with more than 100,000 inhabitants, 8 of which had more than 200,000 inhabitants and 2 more than a million.

At present Spain is going through a period of transition from an agricultural to an industrial structure. The working population is divided as follows: agriculture 39·7% (66·3% in 1900); industry, 32·9%; tertiary sector, 27·3%. However, agriculture contributes only 1·25% to the national income, although it represents 55% of the value of the export trade. In the vast stretches of the Spanish interior cereals are still grown with a biennial rotation of crops and low harvests. The percentage of the population employed in agriculture remains very high and is related to the delay in mechanization; it is tending to decrease with advancing mechanization, the number of tractors having risen from 4300 in 1940 to 93,000 in 1960.

40 per cent of the agricultural population are wage-labourers, the highest rates being paid on the large estates in southern Spain. The latifundium predominates in the south and west and, in general, to the south of the line of the Tagus, whereas in the north, especially in Atlantic Spain, the emphasis is on small farms and on successive parcelling of holdings, which a concentration plan is trying to rectify.

The area of irrigated land has increased by 500,000 ha. in twelve years, thanks to the new projects under the Badajoz Plan and those of the Ebro, the Tagus, and the Guadalquivir. The total area is now more than 2 million ha. (10% of the cultivated land).

Among new crops which have expanded greatly in recent years is cotton, which, in 1962, produced 350,000 tons of raw fibre. Andalusia is the main producing region (50%), followed by Estremadura and the Levante.

The general position as regards stock raising is stationary, with a decrease in the wool-producing breeds; the traditional form of transhumance is in decline, being superseded by the railway for moving stock. On the other hand, the fishing industry has considerably increased and its production plays an important part in Spanish feeding. Spain is one of the countries of Europe and the world where this activity is of greatest importance.

Mining no longer produces the vast wealth of the past, nor is it of much export value. The richest copper, iron, and lead deposits are nearly exhausted. Whereas in the past Spain was the first copper producer, today it can no longer meet the requirements of its own industry.

The situation for iron is better (although the high-grade ores of the Biscay Basin are exhausted and only carbonates remain), and still more so for zinc, sulphur, mercury, and potash. The outlook seems promising for the radio-active minerals.

Coal production is over 15 million tons, but extraction and

transport difficulties increase the cost. So far oil prospecting has not produced any results, but a refining industry has been set up, based on the big Escombreras (Carthagena) refinery, which will soon be able to meet the requirements of the home market. As regards the production of electricity, the figure in 1962 was 22·99 million kWh. (3·957 million in 1940), 30% of which is of thermic origin and the remainder hydraulic.

Industry employs 32·9% of the working population and contributes 30% of the national income.

Steel production reached 2,333,000 tons in 1961. This increase is due to the establishment of steel at Avila (Asturias), which put that region in the forefront of the industry, overtaking Biscay, whose blast furnaces on the Nervion were the largest in Spain.

Cement production, which was more than 6 million tons in 1961, is not yet sufficient to meet the needs of the home market and expanding economy.

The chemical industry has developed considerably during the last twenty years, particularly pharmaceuticals, nitrate fertilizers, and cellulose-base textile fibres from the two large establishments of Torrelavega (Santander) and Miranda de Ebro (Alava), which have commenced exporting. The engineering industry has expanded greatly (rolling-stock, automobile industry in co-operation with foreign firms, motor-cycles, domestic appliances, agricultural machinery). Special mention should be made of shipbuilding, one of the most ancient industries in Spain, with numerous dockyards in the north-west on the Andalusian coast, and in the Levante. These shipyards work not only for Spain but also for some Latin American countries.

The Spanish balance of trade shows a deficit, but the difference between imports and exports is compensated, in the general balance of payments, by receipts from tourism, which amounted in 1963 to 95% of export receipts. The tourist industry began to expand in 1951, when there were 1,263,197 foreign visitors, and its giddy ascent carried the figure in 1963 to 10,031,626, of which 86·5% were from European countries, with France at the top of the list, followed by England and Germany.

PROFESSOR MANUEL TERAN-ALVAREZ
University of Madrid

SWEDEN

General Introduction

During the last hundred years Sweden has developed from being one of the poorest countries in Europe to becoming the one with the highest national per capita income. It has only 7·8 million inhabitants, but an area almost as large as that of Great Britain and Western Germany together. The northern and southern extremities of the country are separated by a distance as great as that between Hamburg and Naples. The bedrock, composed mainly of Primary rocks (granite and gneiss), is resistant and of low relief. In the north-west vast mountain areas rise above tree-level (Kebnekajse, 2123 m.). The country is not subject to natural catastrophes, such as earthquakes, floods, or severe droughts.

Like other formerly glaciated regions, there are many lakes, Lakes Vänern and Vättern being among the largest in Europe. The 'highest coastline' is an important geographical division. Below this level, which is still rising slowly due to post-glacial land-upheaval, lie most of Sweden's clay soils; these are especially suited to agriculture. Above this 'highest coastline' level arable land is restricted to fertile clayey moraines on remnants of sedimentary rocks as in Skåne.

Sweden has a cool, moist climate, governed by the cyclonic activity along the polar front. South-westerly winds bring moist air, warmed by the Gulf Stream. In the south there is snow on the ground for a month every winter, and in the north it lies for as long as eight months; the sea along the Baltic coast north of Stockholm freezes over for a substantial part of the year.

Natural Resources

Sweden is not very richly endowed by nature. Its soils are mostly poor and the climate on the whole is not very favourable to agriculture.

The industrialization of Europe, however, turned the large areas of poor land, covered by coniferous forests (50 % of the total area of Sweden), into a valuable source of raw material. A second important natural resource is the rich iron-ore deposits, the exploitation of which became possible with the development of the Thomas process.

The absence of fuels, such as coal and oil, is however, a serious draw-back that is only partly compensated for by an abundant supply of hydro-electric power.

The export of timber, sawn wood, and iron ore provides the capital for the industrialization of Sweden. The following table illustrates the change:

Distribution of Population according to Branches of Economy

	1850 (%)	1900 (%)	1965 (%)
Agriculture, etc.	78	55	15
Industry, etc.	9	28	43
Trade, service, etc.	13	17	43

Sweden is now a wealthy industrial country, exporting industrial products and capital, but importing raw materials, fuel, and man-power.

In terms of foreign trade per capita Sweden ranks among the world's foremost trading nations.

Population and Settlement

Birth and death rates are low, and the natural growth of population is very slow. The expansion of industry has led to a lack of manpower, with the result that there are now in Sweden a large number of immigrant workers.

Parallel with industrialization, urbanization has spread rapidly. More than 60% of the population live in towns of over 2000 inhabitants. It is the three principal urban zones which have the highest growth rate, but this is achieved at the cost of all the other regions: vast areas, especially in the northern inland regions, are being depopulated. A new socio-economic distribution pattern is emerging.

The only ethnic minority in Sweden, the Lapps, number 10,000, of whom only a small proportion earn their living by breeding reindeer.

In Sweden it is compulsory to attend school for nine years, and there is a liberal system of financial support available for those who wish to pursue higher education,

Stockholm, the capital, owes its importance historically to its favourable position in an administratively centralized Swedish kingdom that formerly included Finland (up to 1809) and other territories around the Baltic. Greater Stockholm, now with more than 1·2 million inhabitants, plays a dominant role in Swedish economic, cultural, and political life. The old part of the city is rich in places of historical interest (medieval and baroque) and is of great natural beauty. The new suburbs are known for their modern town-planning. Like other Swedish towns, Stockholm has no slums.

Göteborg, half a million inhabitants, is the country's largest port and one of the main industrial centres. The fortified Old Town was built to a plan of Dutch origin (seventeenth century).

Malmö, regional capital of southernmost Sweden, one-quarter of a million inhabitants, is situated opposite Copenhagen on the highly urbanized Oresund coast.

Since the land reforms of the eighteenth to nineteenth centuries the old villages have disappeared in most parts of Sweden. Today thousands of farmhouses lie abandoned. But many others have been converted into summer residences.

Geography of Production

All branches of the Swedish economy are undergoing a rapid structural change towards the creation of bigger units, but small units are still common.

Agriculture is highly mechanized, and although it contributes only 4% to the national product, production is sufficient to make Sweden agriculturally self-sufficient. The acreage being worked is shrinking, but output remains fairly steady, thanks to rising productivity. Forest-based industries account for 40% of Sweden's total exports, but are responsible for only 10% of the national product. Most important is the *pulp* and *paper* industry, located on the Norrland coast and in Vänern. Sweden is normally the world's chief exporter of pulp. Forestry is mechanized, and the number of people employed is diminishing rapidly. Timber is taken all the year round to the mills by lorry; only rarely nowadays is it floated downstream to them. The *metal sector* is one of the pillars of the Swedish economy, engineering alone accounting for 40% of the country's industrial production and for 50% of its export. Sweden is probably the world's greatest *iron ore* exporting country; much of the ore is mined in *Kiruna-Gällivare* and exported via Narvik in Norway and Luleå. Kiruna, where the mining is now done underground, alone holds half of Sweden's known deposits. The iron content is very high (64%). The old *Bergslagen* district in middle Sweden has phosphorus-free ores of well-known quality. The mines are integrated with the steel industry of the district. Iron ore is exported from Grängesberg via Oxelösund. Ore deposits other than iron (copper, zinc, lead, silver, gold) are exploited in the *Skellefte* region of Norrland. The famous Falu copper-mine, which once dominated the world copper market, is now exhausted.

Bergslagen, with its rich resources of wood, iron ore, and hydraulic power, is historically the centre of the *steel industry*. Though the use of charcoal in the production of steel has died out, high-quality steel is still an important Swedish export. *Sandviken*, for example, west of Gävle, produces a hard steel (such as is used in drills) that is exported all over the world.

Other big steel plants like *Domnarvet*, *Luleå*, and *Oxelösund* keep the country self-sufficient in ordinary steel.

Engineering dominates the industry of many cities in middle Sweden, such as Stockholm (LM Ericsson electrical equipment, Aflalaval separators), Göteborg (Götaverken shipyard, Volvo cars, SKF ball-bearings), Västerås (ASEA electric plants), Trollhättan (NOHAB locomotives, SAAB cars, and aeroplane engines), Linköping (SAAB cars and aeroplanes), Karlstad (pulp- and paper-mill equipment), Södertälje (Scania-Vabis trucks), Huskvarna (household machines, rifles), Bofors (guns), and Eskilstuna (steel manufacturing, Bolinder-Munktell tractors).

Sweden has a wide range of industries producing *consumer goods*, including food, textiles, radio and television sets, rubber, leather, graphical materials, chemicals. An ever greater part of the rapidly increasing *consumption of energy* must be met by imports (up to 60%) in spite of the maximum exploitation of the water-power resources of the rivers in Norrland.

Half of Sweden's *railway network*, per capita the longest in Europe, is uneconomical, and lines are being closed down. The transport of goods is being carried out increasingly by road, and more and more people now own their cars, the number of which is greater than in any other European country in proportion to the population. The only *inland waterway* of any importance is the Trollhätte canal, connecting Vänern with Göteborg. The old, tiny Göta canal is a tourist route.

Regional Divisions

Administratively, Sweden is divided into *län*, which only partly coincide with the historical *landskap* (provinces). Uppland, for instance, the historical heart of the kingdom (Old Uppsala, dating from the sixth century), is a *landskap*. It is divided into two *län*, one of which also includes part of another *landskap*. The *landskap* are traditionally grouped into Götaland, Svealand, and Norrland.

Geographically, Sweden may be divided into the following regions:

The northern uplands and coast, including the very mountainous area, hilly woodlands dissected by river valleys running west-east, and coastal lowlands. This region is the richest in natural resources of forest, ores, and water-power, but it also includes unpopulated wilderness; its winters are severe. Population and industry are concentrated, apart from inland mining towns and small agricultural areas, on the coast. Iron-ore mines, sawmills, pulp- and paper-mills (Sundsvall-Kramfors district), and electric power-stations are numerous. Agriculture (hay, barley, and potatoes) is rapidly dying out as people 'emigrate' to the south.

Umeå is a cultural centre of Norrland, with the fifth university of Sweden.

The central lowlands, where there are numerous large lakes, is the economic heart of Sweden. The region includes most of the towns (universities in Stockholm, Göteborg, Uppsala), among them the two greatest. The peneplain of old rocks, fragmented by fissures and escarpments, is partly covered with clay and sand (*eskers*).

The eastern part of the region has a good agrarian structure and specializes in cereals; in the western part smallholdings predominate, and milk is a major product.

Fishing is concentrated on the west coast, north of Göteborg (Bohuslän).

Engineering forms the basis of the economy, but textiles (Borås, Norrköping), pulp and paper (Väner basin), shoemaking (Örebro), oil-refining (Göteborg, Nynäshamn), and petrochemical products (Stenungssund) are also important.

The southern uplands, with plateaux up to 200–350 m., is a wooded region where have been developed small, numerous, but mostly very modern and enterprising industries. Some are famous for their glassware, furniture, or prefabricated houses; others supply the Swedish market with modern designed products in wood, leather, metal, and plastics. The expansion of light industry absorbs the drift of workers away from agriculture, which is about to disappear from this region of poor, stony soils.

The southern coasts and lowlands, including Öland and Gotland, have the longest growing season, good soils, and the most diversified agricultural production (wheat, sugar beet, barley, vegetables, fruit, pigs, and cattle); Skåne has the main food-processing industries, including deep freezing.

New big paper-mills exploit the fast-growing forests. Western Skåne is a rapidly growing industrial area, including many branches of production based on imported raw materials. Local low-grade coal and clay are used for potteries and brick-making.

The traffic across the Öresund is heavy, and the building of a bridge is under discussion.

Geographically the southern provinces form a transition to Central Europe. They bear many marks of their having been part of the Danish kingdom until three hundred years ago.

Lund is an old cultural centre, once seat of the Danish archbishop, and now a university town.

PROFESSOR STAFFAN HELMFRID
Head of Department of Human Geography
University of Stockholm

SWITZERLAND

[Unless otherwise stated, only statistics of the year 1960 are used. More statistics will be found in the *Schweizer Brevier*, which is published every year in German and French.]

Geographical Situation

Switzerland is a small country in the centre of Europe with an area of 41,388 sq. km. The frontiers have remained unchanged since the Congress of Vienna (1815) and are very long (1885 km.) in comparison to the area. For the most part they are natural frontiers determined by mountains and rivers.

The country has no access to the high seas, with long distances to the major European ports (644 km. to Marseilles, 830 km. to Rotterdam). This increases the cost of transport of raw materials and foodstuffs, which in turn accounts for the high cost of living.

Switzerland has been called the 'turntable of Europe'. In particular its many Alpine passes have enormous economic significance.

It is in the northern temperate zone, between 46° and 48°N. The influence of the Alps as a climatic boundary results in greater climatic differences than its north–south extent of 220 km. would suggest.

Structure

Switzerland may be divided into three main regions: the Alps, the Mittelland, and the Jura, with 60%, 30%, and 10% of the total area respectively. Considering the general physiogeographical structure, we may call it an Alpine country.

The Alps. Within the European Alps the Swiss ones are noted for their height, especially to the west of the tectonic boundary (Lake Constance, Chur, Splügen, Como) which separates the Western from the Eastern Alps. They are sparsely populated with the exception of the sunny terraces and large glacial valleys. Eighteen per cent of the Alpine region is forested.

The Mittelland. Alluvial land with glacial deposits. It extends to the east of Lake Constance as the Schwäbisch-Bayerische Hochebene. Infertile sandstones are covered by fertile morainic detritus. Agriculture and industry are concentrated here and maintain 60% of the total population. Larger towns and prosperous villages connected by a dense road and rail network characterize this part of the country.

The Jura are much lower and of simpler structure than the Alps. Long drawn-out folds alternate with synclinal valleys and intersecting *cluses*. Towards France the Jura have a plateau character. In the north we find tilted block-mountains. The valleys and the zone near the Mittelland are fairly densely populated.

Rivers and Lakes

Rivers come down from the Alps in all directions. They have steep gradients and are largely unsuited as routes of communication. When the snow begins to melt there is danger of flooding. Lakes, 3 % of the total area, are very important for traffic and tourism.

Natural Resources

Switzerland is geologically speaking a young country with no important mineral deposits. The small coal deposits are mined only in wartime. Here and there iron ores are exploited, but are exported down the Rhine owing to the lack of coal. A small asphalt deposit is exploited by a British firm (Val Travers) in the Jura. The limestones and sandstones are used as building materials. Switzerland is also self-sufficient in salt. At present several attempts are being made to find oil in the Mittelland.

Hydro-electric power. To compensate for her lack of mineral resources, Switzerland has abundant hydro-electric power at her disposal. The main power stations lie in the Alps and on the large rivers of the Mittelland. There are many artificial lakes in the Alps.

Climate

Over a relatively small area, Switzerland has a very diversified climate. Switzerland lies in the transition zone between the continental and oceanic climates of Europe. In addition the Alps are also a climatic boundary. To the south we have the mild, sunny Mediterranean climate. To the north westerly winds, under the influence of the Gulf Stream, result in the annual mean temperature being 5°C. higher than its geographical position would suggest. Nevertheless temperatures are determined largely by the height.

The annual rainfall is between 60 and 400 cm. and shows an increase from east to west. The windward sides of the mountains have a particularly high rainfall. The western part of the Mittelland

and many Alpine valleys are rather dry. The southern part of Switzerland has its precipitation maximum in autumn (like north Italy), whereas the northern areas have a summer maximum. The climate is particularly important for the Alpine resorts, such as Arosa, Davos, Montana, and so on, which have a so-called high Alpine climate (sunny and dry).

Vegetation

About a quarter of the total area is covered by forests. The Alps and the Jura are particularly densely wooded. In the lower parts there are deciduous trees and conifers. Higher up there are beech trees, common spruce, and larch. Coniferous forests end at about 1800 m., in the Central Alps at 2200 m.

Population

In 1850 Switzerland had 2·4 million inhabitants, a hundred years later 4·7 million, in 1960 5·5 million, and in 1966 nearly 6 million. This represents 145 inhabitants per sq. km. over-all; in the permanently settled areas 250 inhabitants per sq. km.

Urban population (communities with over 10,000 inhabitants) was 42% in 1960, 33% in 1940, and 6% in 1850.

In 1960 there were 585,000 foreigners living in Switzerland, in addition to 721,000 foreign workers (1964), mostly Italians.

The number of Swiss abroad (including dual-nationals) is 255,000. Since 1930, however, fewer and fewer Swiss have been settling abroad.

In the course of a long and varied history many different peoples have intermixed in Switzerland—Rhäts, Celts, Romans, Burgundians, and differing Germanic tribes. This is borne out by the great diversity in the spoken languages:

German speaking 69·3%
French speaking 18·9%
[1]Italian speaking   9·5%
Romance speaking 0·9%

In addition to these written languages there are countless local dialects, especially in the German-speaking parts of the country.

---

[1] The number of Italian speakers doubled in the ten years from 1950 to 1960.

Economic Structure

The land available for agricultural use has been unable to support the growing population, and this has forced the country to industrialize. Today nearly half of the working population is employed by industry or in building trades.

Agriculture

Only 10% is employed in agriculture. Nevertheless the two World Wars have shown the importance for a neutral country with no access to the high seas of maintaining its agricultural production. The State assists farming through subsidies and price guarantees. An increase in mechanization makes up for shortage of labour. In former times grain was of foremost importance. Competition from abroad has forced a transfer to cattle breeding and milk products.

The relatively small amount of precipitation and the increase of the urban population have favoured this development.

Switzerland can cover her own needs in milk, butter, cheese, meat, eggs, potatoes, and vegetables, but her own grain production would suffice for only eight months in the year.

Industry

Switzerland is one of the oldest industrial countries of Europe. Despite unfavourable conditions, industry has become the most important economic mainstay of the country.

Her own market is unable to absorb even half of the industrial output. Export of industrial products is discouraged by long and expensive transit costs. Switzerland must thus concentrate on high-quality goods that need few raw materials and abundant labour, and whose transport costs are low in comparison with production costs. The machine, metal, watch, textile, and clothing industries are well-known. Swiss watches worth more than 1500 million francs are exported to sixty countries.

The main industrial centres are situated in the Mittelland between Zürich and Lake Constance, the Aare Valley, in the valleys of the Jura, and all the big towns.

In 1960, 50% of the working population was employed in industry. Industrial production accounts for about one-third of the national income.

Tourism

Besides agriculture and industry, tourism is of special economic significance. People from all over the world visit the many mountains, lakes, and the sunny Ticino, either for Alpine sports (skiing, mountaineering) or just for a restful family holiday. The number of foreign visitors is nearly twice as great as that of home visitors. Tourists from Germany, France, Italy, the Benelux countries, and the USA are especially numerous.

Road and Rail Traffic

Because of its central position, sandwiched between large countries of different cultural and economic regions, Switzerland has been an important transit link ever since Roman times. Various passes were followed by the great railway tunnels (Gotthard, Simplon, Lötschberg). Today road tunnels are being built. The road and rail network is especially dense in the Mittelland. The railways are mainly nationalized and are practically 100 % electric. At present a network of motorways is being built.

Waterways

The coming of the railways was the death of the inland waterways (with the exception of the large lakes). Ever since the beginning of the twentieth century, however, the great Rhine waterway from Holland to Basle has increased its economic importance from year to year. In 1963 Basle was the third largest inland port on the Rhine, with an annual turnover of more than eight million tons.

Import Goods, Annual Average 1955-64

Coal	1,609,000 tons
Oil	1,740,000 tons
Cereals	609,000 tons
Metals	883,000 tons

Only 5 % of all the goods transported goes downstream.

New projects are planned to extend this waterway to Lake Constance, to connect the Rhine with the Rhône, and to connect Lago Maggiore with the Po, in Italy.

To improve the economic ties with overseas, the Swiss high-seas fleet was inaugurated in 1941. In 1964 it consisted of thirty vessels of 161,000 net reg. tons.

Air Traffic

Switzerland has three international airports—Zürich, Basle, and Geneva, in addition to a local airport at Berne.

Foreign Trade

In relation to its population, Switzerland has one of the largest trade turnovers in the world. A very important part of all industrial production is exported. About 50% of all foodstuffs and about 90% of all raw materials are imported. The most important trade partners are the Federal Republic of Germany, France, Italy, and the USA.

Mean Annual Value of Export Goods for the Period 1962–64 in Million Francs

Metal industry	5,645
including watches alone	1,519
Chemical and pharmaceutical industry	2,027
Textile industry	1,135
Food, drink, and luxury industry	541
including cheese alone	170

Values of Exports to Some Foreign Countries, in Percentage of the Whole Export
(Mean values for the period 1960–64)

Federal Republic of Germany	17·2
United States of America	9·4
Italy	9·0
France	8·0
Austria	3·6
EEC countries	41·0
EFTA countries	18·0

(100% = 9·687 million francs)

The value of imports, especially foods and raw materials, is 20 to 25% higher than that of the exports. The trade gap is offset by earnings from the tourist trade and transit traffic, in addition to the earnings of Swiss firms and capital abroad.

Political Structure

Switzerland is a republic. The Swiss Confederation is made up of twenty-two cantons, of which three are further divided up into half cantons—Appenzell, Basel, and Unterwalden. Each of these twenty-five states has its own constitution and civil-law code. They have representatives in the *Bundesversammlung* (Federal Assembly), which is responsible for federal matters and which elects the executive body, the Council of Ministers (*Bundesrat*).

Switzerland is neutral. To maintain her neutrality she possesses a militia for which all able-bodied men between 20 and 50 years of age are eligible for service.

Thanks to her central position and political stability, Switzerland has become the home of several international organizations, such as the Red Cross, the World Postal Union, the International Labour Organization, and the Bank for International Settlements.

DR HANS BERNHARD
Professor an der Kantonschule
Zürich

TURKEY

INTRODUCTION: LOCATION AND CULTURAL BACKGROUND

Geographical location, together with the physical setting and historical background of the country, is the most important factor which has helped to shape the cultural, social, and economic aspects of Turkey, as well as her political affiliations in the past and present.

Dual Character: a Country of Europe and Asia

Turkey is the easternmost member country of the Council of Europe. Her area (780,600 sq. km.) is greater than that of the United Kingdom, the Federal Republic of Germany, and Italy combined. Turkish territories lie in the middle of the Old World, partly in Europe (23,600 sq. km.; approximately four-fifths of the area of Belgium or Holland) and partly in Asia (757,000 sq. km.; larger than France and the Benelux countries together). Hence the dual character of Turkey; it is a European and an Asiatic country at the same time.

The duality of Turkey is, however, not only territorial. It is deeply rooted in the historical and cultural background of the country. Indeed, the area known as Turkey has long been a link between oriental and occidental realms of culture. Traditional routes to the east and west for both invaders and traders crossed Turkey throughout history. Central Anatolia, the core of the country, was inhabited by Hittites at the dawn of history and they also controlled the margins. Their contacts included both Babylonia and Egypt. Then came waves of invaders from the west (*e.g.*, Phrygians, Lydians, Greeks, Macedonians) and the east (*e.g.*, Persians). In the last centuries B.C. Turkey was materially and culturally one of the most advanced areas of Western civilization. Many industrial settlements were busily making cloth, carpets, pottery, wines, and wares of bronze, gold, silver, and iron. The central parts were a granary of the ancient world and exported cereals and animal products. The whole country, especially the coastal regions, continued to prosper during Roman times; but there followed a general decline during the Byzantine period. This was succeeded by the last human influx from the East which resulted in the settlement of the area by the Turks, who gave their name, their language, and their religion to the country. They founded the Seljuk State and the Turkish (Ottoman) Empire. At its peak the Turkish Empire included practically the whole of south-eastern Europe, the coastal areas around the Black Sea, and the Near East, with the exception of Iran. After some centuries came the long period of decline which ended at the end of the First World War in the rebirth of Turkey and the foundation of the present Turkish Republic on the homeland of the former Empire.

These events contributed in a large measure to the exchange of culture and of goods between East and West and led to considerable population displacements, especially between the homeland and the Balkan countries, during the periods of expansion and decline. Combined with the natural setting of the country, they have largely influenced the cultural pattern of present Turkey. Indeed, the country now combines specifically Turkish traditions from Central Asia with elements of Islam, inherited traditions of older cultures indigenous to the country, and those of the modern Western world. It is therefore understandable that Turkey has often been called a 'bridge' between East and West, a country where 'orient and occident meet'.

Turkey is, at the same time, a Near Eastern country. She occupies a marginal part of the Near East, but is clearly distinguished from the rest of the region, both physically and culturally. Indeed, the country forms to the north of the extensive Arabian platform a mountainous block of land about 1500 km. long and 600 km. wide. There are no deserts. Semi-arid conditions and steppe vegetation occur only in the central and south-eastern parts, whereas the rest of it falls within the limits of semi-arid or even humid climates with natural forest vegetation. From the standpoint of human geography it forms the south-eastern continuation of the great European agglomeration. It is true that the country is—in general—less densely inhabited (density of population 40 per sq. km.) than in neighbouring areas to the west. But essentially it belongs to the same agglomeration since there is no break in between. Besides, the patterns of settlement and land-use are characterized by continuity. The country possesses a relatively well-developed network of railways and shows a great similarity to the countries of southern and south-eastern Europe in many aspects of economic life, whereas east and south of Turkey one enters the proper realm of the Arid Zone where extensive deserts prohibit continuous settlement and bring about drastic changes in land-use pattern, communication systems, and the general way of life.

A Block between Eastern Europe and the Mediterranean

The east–west extension of the Anatolian mountain block has resulted in a sharp separation of two cultural realms—Slavic or East European to the north and Mediterranean and Oriental to the south. At its peak the Turkish Empire extended from the northern Black Sea coasts to the shores of the Red Sea. But even at that time the rugged mountain block of Anatolia acted as a barrier between the two regions, and the main social, economic, and cultural exchanges tended to take place between the homeland and its western and southern areas. This led to a sharp isolation of the two geographical regions to the north and south of the country.

The Anatolian mountain barrier is interrupted only by the narrow and easily controlled Straits (the Bosporus, the Sea of Marmara, and the Dardanelles). It is through this natural passage way that the link between the Black Sea and the Mediterranean countries had been established in ancient Greek and Byzantine times, and today the Straits are one of the principal maritime passages of the world. The strategic importance of the situation on the Straits is obvious, since it enables Turkey to 'bottle up' the Black Sea basin. In fact, it has enabled Turkey to prevent Russian expansion into the Mediterranean. The control of the Straits has been therefore a means of political power. But at times it was also a source of international conflict.

Effects of Europeanization

The historical background also explains the origins of revolutionary efforts at Europeanization during the last forty years, a distinguishing feature of present-day Turkey as compared with other Moslem countries of the Near East. The Caliphate was abolished, schools and social life were secularized, a programme of compulsory primary education was initiated. The Roman alphabet was adopted, and European legal codes replaced the old Moslem law. Women were emancipated by altering a long Turkish tradition, and political suffrage was made universal. As a result of these social changes and a parallel programme of economic development which attempted to rush through centuries of Western evolution within a short time, Turkey, for long balanced between East and West, definitely entered the Western orbit, a fact which is reflected in her close political economic and cultural co-operation with the European countries. But it must not be forgotten that Turkey's significance still lies equally in her own rich cultural heritage and her Eastern affiliations.

NATURAL SETTING

Relief

Turkey is included in the Alpine mountain system and forms a recently upwarped area having a mean altitude of 1100 m. Steep slopes are a characteristic feature. Altitude increases eastward to an average of 2000 m. in eastern Anatolia, the roof of the country, where even many depressions lie at a height of over 2000 m. Thus great altitude is one of the most important factors affecting climate, vegetation, settlement, agriculture, and social and economic development. It also accounts for the striking differences between high inland and low coastal areas.

Recent lavas cover large areas in central and eastern Turkey, and the highest mountain, Agri (or Ararat, 5165 m.), is of volcanic origin. Nevertheless the orographic features of Turkey are dominated by high marginal mountains in the north and south, running east–west. They owe their origin to Alpine folds and rise locally above 3500 or even 4000 m. They are composed of parallel ranges separated by deep valleys and depressions, and encircle the plateau of central Anatolia by forming two mountain knots to the east and west of it.

This arrangement of landforms has various consequences:

(*a*) The formation of an interior basin in the central part of the country.

(*b*) The formation of longitudinal or subsequent valleys between the parallel ranges and relatively few transverse gorges cutting through the marginal mountains. Transverse gorges owe their origin either to superimposition or recent capture.

(*c*) The formation of a fretted and island-girt shoreline in the west which differs markedly from the longitudinal coasts of the Black Sea and the Mediterranean. Uneven distribution of rainfall, humid, even extremely humid, exterior slopes in the marginal areas; exaggerated rain-shadow effects on the lee sides and the generally semi-arid character of the central part.

(*d*) Sharp differences in temperature regimes between coastal areas and the interior. In the coastal areas the annual temperature range (17°–20°C.) is small, and the number of days with frost or snow cover is few. Along the Mediterranean snowfall is unusual, and the occurrence of sharp frosts very rare (frequency of occurrence of −5° and −10°C., less than every 20 years and 100 years, respectively). In the interior the temperature range is great (25°–30°C.), snow and frost are usual in winter, and temperatures may fall below −30°C. The duration of continuous snow cover varies between 1 and 4 months. Hence the sharp differences in soils, vegetation, settlement types, and agriculture between the centre and the margins.

Climate

Turkey is situated in the transition zone between the core of the tropical air masses to the south and that of polar air masses to the north. The climatic conditions of the country are determined by the seasonal changes in the areal extent of these two systems and of the location of polar front and associated cyclonic activities. The country is therefore hot and usually dry in summer, the two exceptions being the orographic rains on the exterior slopes of the northern marginal mountains and convectional precipitation on the north-eastern plateaux. On the other hand, the country is subjected to the influences of the polar front in winter and receives abundant precipitation due to increased frontal and cyclonic activities.

Four climatically different regions may be distinguished in Turkey:

> (a) Eastern Black Sea (in the north): warm summers, mild winters, precipitation in all seasons.
> (b) Mediterranean: hot, dry summers, and mild, wet winters.
> (c) Continental: warm summers, very cold winters, sufficient precipitation at all seasons.
> (d) Semi-arid: cold and humid winters, hot summers.

They owe their origin to differences in location and in degree of continentality and altitude, in addition to the modification induced by orographic features. Hence we find great variety in local climatic types from almost tropical to taiga and tundra on the one side and from semi-arid to extremely humid on the other.

Natural Vegetation and Soils

Semi-arid central and south-eastern Anatolia are steppe regions, whereas the rest of Turkey falls climatically within an area of natural forest. Present forest, however, covers less than a fifth of the country as a result of intense deforestation during the long period of land occupance.

Four vegetation regions can be distinguished. They are both floristically and physiologically different:

(a) The Black Sea region. Most densely wooded and floristically richest part of the country, characterized by lush colchic forest in the east.

(b) Region of Mediterranean vegetation (maquis, deciduous and coniferous forests).

(c) Steppe region in central and south-eastern Anatolia.

(d) Region of coniferous forest (taiga) in the cold continental uplands of the north-east.

Alluvial soils cover a relatively small area in Turkey (approximately 6%). Zonal soils prevail and show great variety. In the humid marginal regions they are usually podzolic or lateritic, whereas reddish-brown and grey steppe soils prevail in the semiarid interior.

POPULATION AND SETTLEMENT

The human geography of Turkey reflects characteristic features of a prevailingly agricultural country with striking regional inequalities in economic structure and stage of development.

Population Density

Turkey's population has almost trebled within forty years (in 1927, 13·6 millions, in 1965, 32·4 millions). The rate of population growth is very high (25‰). This presents one of the most important problems of the country.

The arithmetic density is 40 per sq. km., and Turkey may thus be regarded as a country of intermediate density. However, both physiological and agricultural densities are among the highest in Europe and reach 126 and 100 per sq. km. of cultivated land, respectively. From this point of view Turkey may be regarded as an overpopulated country and the living standard of her people low by Western standards. Overpopulation depends, however, largely on the current level of technological development. Hence the need for and the adoption of a development plan covering many fields of the country's demographic, social, cultural, and economic problems.

General Distribution

(*a*) The general pattern of population distribution is characterized by concentration in four more or less continuous areas—the coastal region along the eastern Black Sea; the region around the Sea of Marmara, including Thrace; the Aegean region; and a relatively smaller area around the Gulf of Iskenderun. In the last three areas, which are relatively more developed and economically diversified, density approaches 80 to 100 persons per sq. km.

As to the eastern Black Sea coasts, these form an over-populated area with a dominantly agricultural population and a density exceeding 200 locally.

The semi-arid interior and south-east, as well as most of the mountainous Mediterranean region, are less densely inhabited. Lowest densities occur in the cold, high, and rugged uplands of the east.

(*b*) In detail, population distribution is often characterized by a linear pattern due to a parallel arrangement of agriculturally valuable lands along valleys, plains, and depressions (the effect of the landforms).

Rural Distribution

(*a*) Three-fourths of Turkey's active population is engaged in agriculture. Hence the prevalence of rural settlements and low, though increasing, urbanization. Agglomerated villages are the dominant type. Dispersed rural settlements occur mainly in the humid north, along the Black Sea.

(*b*) True nomadism with extensive horizontal displacements, a feature occurring in many areas of the country even in the nineteenth century, has been virtually eliminated as a result of a successful policy of settlement and colonization, mainly in the second half of the nineteenth century, and as a result of territorial changes after the first World War. But vertical nomadism (transhumance) is still practised in many mountainous areas.

Urban Distribution

(*a*) The percentage of urban population is relatively high in the more developed and economically diversified west and north-west, and in the sub-region around the Gulf of Iskenderun. Most cities are located in these regions and on the periphery of central Anatolia.

(b) Turkey is characterized by a relatively high percentage (34%) of functionally agricultural towns of medium size. Manufacturing cities rank next (28%) and include the most important cities of the country such as Istanbul (1,750,000), and Izmir (417,000), Adana (290,000), Bursa (212,000), Eskisehir (175,000); Ankara (902,000, the capital and the second largest city) has a rather complex character. Altogether, fourteen cities exceed the 100,000 mark.

ECONOMIC ASPECTS

Introduction

Throughout the ages agriculture has been the most important branch of the economy. This also remains true for Turkey today. Although remarkable developments have taken place in mining and manufacturing during recent decades, 75% of the active population is still engaged in agriculture, whereas those occupied in mining and manufacturing represent only 7·4%, and agricultural products constitute 90% of exports by value.

In general, the per capita income in Turkey is low (in 1963 about $216 a year, non-active population included), and the living standard of her people is below that of the West. But the country possesses considerable potentialities which, when developed, should provide much better living conditions for a rapidly increasing population.

Regional Differences: Recent Developments

Turkey is characterized by great differences in economic structure and inequalities of economic development. Sharp contrasts exist, especially between the west and east on one side and the interior and marginal areas on the other. Agriculture is diversified and considerably mechanized, and most of the manufacturing is located in the west, whereas animal husbandry is—in general—the main occupation in the eastern regions. Interior and coastal areas differ markedly. Except for animal products, the interior provides little towards foreign trade, but its cereal surplus feeds the Turkish people. Coastal margins, on the other hand, provide the export crops that are the chief source of Turkey's income, and these areas are characterized by a great variety of products, the fruit of a technologically advanced agriculture. All these factors lead to great regional differences in the distribution of national income and considerable inequalities in living standards.

The desire for a better living standard has led Turkey to set up a State planning organization for revising and organizing her economy and for the utilization of her potential resources at a high technological level.

The need for quick development was realized many years ago, and this has resulted in the considerable extension of agricultural land, the attempts to modernize agriculture, the increased variety of agricultural exports, the construction of a large number of dams for flood control, irrigation, and supply of energy, the construction of new highways and ports, and remarkable achievements in mining and manufacturing. Consequently, per capita income has risen from $50 in 1948 to $216 in 1963 (at constant prices and including non-active population).

Agriculture

Turkey has more than doubled her agricultural lands within the last few decades. They now account for 32% of the country. But one-third of it, mainly in the semi-arid interior, lies fallow every year. Nervertheless the lands actually cultivated cover more than 170,000 sq. km., which is larger than the areas of the Benelux countries and Denmark combined. Meadows and other pasturelands, used mainly for feeding animals, are even more extensive (37% of the country, an area practically as large as Italy).

As a result Turkey now produces more than 16 million tons of cereals annually, in addition to great quantities of industrial crops, fruits, and considerable amounts of raw materials derived from animal husbandry. By far the largest part of the cereals is consumed within the country, whereas considerable quantities of the industrial crops (cotton, tobacco) and fruits (grapes, hazel nuts, figs, olive oil) and animal raw materials are exported.

More than half of the Turkish cereal production is wheat, and with an average production of 8 million tons annually Turkey ranks among the most important producers. More than 50% of the cultivated area is in wheat. The percentage is even higher in the interior. Wheat is the main staple food of the population, except on the humid eastern Black Sea coast, where it is replaced by maize. Its role in foreign trade is unimportant.

Owing to varieties of climate, industrial crops are of many kinds, and cotton, tobacco, sesame, and opium poppy are the most important exports. Together with the dried fruits, such as raisins, figs, hazel nuts, they provide two-thirds of the export by value. Two major agricultural regions may be distinguished—(a) the interior, with prevailing grain production (wheat and barley) and stock-raising. Except for animal products, it contributes little to foreign trade, but its surplus feeds the Turkish people; (b) the coastal margins characterized by a more diversified agriculture and production of export crops.

Minerals

Turkey is characterized by the diversity of her mineral wealth and her remarkable achievements in mining in recent decades. Coal, lignite, chrome, iron, copper, sulphur, oil, and a variety of minerals such as boracite, emery, lead, zinc, mercury, and salt are found. Coal from the Zonguldak field along the western Black Sea coast is the country's major mineral resource and is the richest in the whole eastern Mediterranean. Most of the production is consumed by gigantic steel-mills in near-by Eregli and Karabük. Coal production is around six million tons annually, and reserves appear adequate to meet domestic demands for many years, but growing national requirements hinder export. Chrome leads in export, and Turkey is one of the most important suppliers of the world market. It is followed by ores of copper and manganese, and by boracite. Oil, a new feature in mineral wealth, is increasingly produced, but production (1 million tons) is still far below the domestic need. The chief oilfields are located in the south-east.

Industry

The country has been attempting to effect a quick industrialization in recent years, and the results have already considerably influenced the economic structure of the country. In 1948 agriculture and industries provided 53·2% and 10·5% of the national income respectively. In 1963 the figures were 41·6% and 16·0%. Thus Turkey, at the turn of the century an exclusively agricultural country, is now in possession of highly diversified manufacturing industries, including various branches of the heavy metallurgical and chemical industries.

M

Foreign Trade

European countries outside the Eastern *bloc* have been the main trade partners of Turkey. Among them the Federal Republic of Germany ranks first (roughly 20% of foreign trade by value), followed by the United Kingdom, France, Italy, the Benelux countries, and others in decreasing order. Exchanges with these countries together make up more than two-thirds of Turkish foreign trade by value. The only non-European country playing an important role is the United States of America (slightly more than 20%). It is therefore not surprising that Turkey has been interested in, and has joined, many international economic organizations in Europe such as OEEC (Organization for European Economic Co-operation), in 1961 replaced by OECD (Organization for Economic Development and Co-operation), EPU (European Payments Union), IBRD (International Bank of Reconstruction and Development), EEC (European Economic Community) popularly known as the European Common Market.

SIRRI ERINÇ
Professor of Geography
University of Istanbul

UNITED KINGDOM

The United Kingdom occupies nearly four-fifths of the British Isles, being made up of Great Britain, Northern Ireland, and many island groups or single islands. It has about the same area as the Federal Republic of Germany and less than half that of France. The British Isles are detached parts of continental Europe, rising above an extensive continental shelf, with semi-enclosed seas lying around or between them. The seas around them are so shallow that if their beds rose some 100 m. Britain would be joined to France and the Low Countries and land bridges would join the two major islands, Britain and Ireland.

Within the British Isles there are two distinct states—the United Kingdom and the Republic of Ireland, known as Ireland or Eire. There are also at least four distinguishable national groups—the English, the Scots, the Irish, and the Welsh, each with some degree of cultural distinctness, the result of historical forces which have operated in the different environments of the small but physically variegated British Isles.

Geographical Position

The westerly location of the British Isles long proved a disadvantage: they lay on the outer edge of the known world and received new currents of culture late. Insularity, however, offered certain advantages, especially when the inhabitants of the British Isles, notably the English, could defend their coasts by naval power in the narrow seas. With the opening up of the Atlantic to navigation and with the discovery of the Americas, the British Isles came to occupy a very advantageous position, so that today both for sea and air routes Britain is a very important European terminal.

Climate

The climate of the British Isles is more favourable to agriculture and human activity than their latitude (50°–62° N.) might suggest: most of the country lies north of France, and the Shetland Islands in the extreme north lie north of the latitude of Leningrad and Oslo. Generally, the country has winters that are cool rather than cold, summers warm rather than hot, and precipitation (nearly all rain) which is sufficient for crops, forests, industry, domestic, and other needs.

Landforms and Relief

Great Britain, the major unit of the British Isles, has zones of both highland and lowland country. In Scotland highlands, standing mainly between 400 and 1400 m., occupy the greater part of the country, the lowlands (below 200 m.) lying in central Scotland between the Scottish Highlands and the Southern Uplands and also marginally to the highlands especially along the east coast. In southern Britain the highland zones lie in the west and in the north, but lowlands (often scarplands) are much more extensive. The whole of the United Kingdom has well-developed river systems; many of these invite access inland from the sea to seaports sited at or below their estuary heads as they have also provided riverside sites for many towns; in the highland zones, however, the rivers are little navigable, though also less polluted and thus useful for fishing. The Clyde and Forth in Scotland, and the Thames, Mersey, Humber, and Severn in England are particularly important for their maritime commerce.

Several points, in relation to the landforms, should be underlined. First, England commands the greatest proportion of lowland; this has moderate rainfall and warmer summers and a range of useful soils; it thus had and has the best opportunities for agriculture and settlement. Second, the coal measures lie marginally between the highland and lowland zones, alike in Wales, England, and Scotland. Third, the lowlands have resources of low-grade iron ore and materials for the making of bricks and cement. Fourth, although Great Britain is not of large scale, its physical diversification created a variety of habitats where cultural traits have in some measure survived; thus Welsh and Gaelic speech survive, respectively in Wales and western Scotland, although Cornish, another Celtic speech, has died out and little Manx is still spoken in the Isle of Man; similarly, Scotland has preserved its own system of law, education, and religion.

Vegetation

Woodlands once covered virtually the whole of the British Isles, but now occupy only a very small fraction of the country. Today efforts are made to reafforest with quickly growing conifers mainly highland country, but in the lowlands woods are small, although to be seen almost everywhere since trees decorate parklands and shelter fields and farmhouses.

Population

The population of the United Kingdom numbered 52·7 millions at the census of 1961 and continues to grow slowly at an annual rate of 0·6 %. This last figure takes account of a small but steady flow of emigrants from Britain and of controlled immigration into it of aliens and Commonwealth citizens, chiefly from the Irish Republic. The United Kingdom clearly, despite its small size, supports a remarkably high density of population thanks to its highly industrial and commercial economy. The population is very unevenly distributed; moreover, its rate of growth is quite different in the major parts of the United Kingdom. Thus Scotland and Wales, because of emigration and movement chiefly into England, have populations which are numerically stable: Wales—1951 2·60 millions, 1961 2·64 millions; Scotland—1951 5·10 millions, 1961 5·18 millions. In contrast, England increased its numbers during this decade from 41·2 millions to 43·4 millions and Northern Ireland from 1·37 millions to 1·43 millions. If the increase in England is looked at more closely it is found to have occurred very largely in south-east England, in a diagonal zone between Lancashire and Greater London, around and beyond which workers have moved to higher-paid employment. This trend is likely to continue, especially if economic association with the Continent becomes closer. To meet it three new major towns are to be built in the south-east and many existing towns are to be greatly expanded. Alike within all the major divisions of the United Kingdom, population density differs sharply, from that on bleak uplands to that on agricultural land, and to industrial regions including the coalfields.

Settlements

It is characteristic of the United Kingdom that it is highly urbanized: rather more than four-fifths of the population live in towns of different sizes and functions. Rural depopulation to the advantage of towns and their suburbs has been characteristic in Britain since 1850, when railways introduced a new mobility.

Some towns, such as Chester and York, have grown on sites first chosen during the Roman occupation; many others are relatively new—e.g., Birmingham, Liverpool, and Manchester—in that they have grown vastly since the Industrial Revolution; an increasing number, as for example Harlow and Crawley, are New Towns of quite recent planned origin: eight have been built to house the 'overspill' of London's population; there are others elsewhere in England, in South Wales, and in Scotland. In England too first appeared the 'conurbation' so-called: of those now officially recognized, there are six in England and one in Scotland (Central Clydeside), where urban growth, associated with industrial expansion and population increase, has taken place from a major town (London, Birmingham, Glasgow) or between a group of towns, as in West Yorkshire, Merseyside, and south-east Lancashire. The most populous of these—Greater London—contains between one-fifth and a quarter of England's population. Beyond the towns the countryside is studded with rural settlements which are characteristically scattered farms in upland Wales and no less markedly compact villages in many parts of lowland England.

The Economy

The inhabitants of the United Kingdom enjoy a high standard of living: in 1964 they stood in this respect eleventh in the world and sixth in Europe. The fact that this is achieved for such a large population occupying a relatively small territory reflects the degree to which this country has developed a highly successful industrial and commercial economy. It clearly commands efficient entrepreneur and managerial staffs and skilled workers comparable with those of western Europe generally. However, agriculture is also highly developed.

Agriculture

Only about 6% of the workers are employed on the land. This is a mark of the efficiency of British agriculture, which is highly mechanized, 'capital-intensive', and gives high yields per man-hour. But it still means that Britain depends on overseas suppliers for a large part of its food requirements, especially grain and meat. The principal crops grown—for food, drink, and fodder—are barley, wheat, oats, and potatoes. Some sugar beet, many hard and soft fruits, and vegetables are also found. Glasshouse cultivation (which is protected by tariffs and import quotas) provides large supplies of tomatoes, cucumbers, lettuces, etc., as well as flowers. The emphasis is put throughout most of the British Isles on grassland farming to produce animal products—meat, bacon, milk, cream, butter, cheese, wool, and hides. Arable farming is usually 'mixed'—that is, food and fodder grains are rotated with grass, clover, and root crops grown for fodder. Livestock numbers are relatively high and include a good deal of factory-produced poultry. Despite the dense population of the United Kingdom, which is mainly urban (including suburban), and despite the fact that it is subsidized from Government funds, agriculture cannot meet more than about half of domestic needs for temperate foodstuffs. Thus the country provides a large market for foodstuffs, as also for agricultural raw materials.

While farming has regard to market conditions and to Government policy, it is still also related to the range of environments offered. The lowland east, for example, with summer sun and only moderate rain, is suited to cereals and fruit, with potatoes in the Fens and glasshouse cultivation near London. Sheep farming is more common in the hill country of the north and west, with summer grazing in the highlands; cattle and dairy still predominate in the wetter west, and there are early vegetables and flowers from the Scilly Isles and Cornwall. Whatever the type of farming, a feature of the countryside is the pattern of irregularly shaped fields of varying sizes usually enclosed in the lowlands by hedgerows and in the uplands by low dry-stone walls.

A continuing and serious problem of agricultural concern is the steady loss of agricultural land to industrial and urban development —about 400,000 ha. per decade. While on balance some land is steadily gained from the sea and from industrial waste land, this problem has to be solved by more efficient use of existing lands: thus attention is turned to improvement of extensive hill and rough grazing lands (above 240 m.), by the reclamation of coastal marshes ('saltings')—which also provide much needed water resources—by irrigation of certain free-percolating but otherwise poor soils, and by the increasing use of selected strains of grass and grains, fertilizers, and new means of pest and disease control.

Fisheries

The United Kingdom makes good use of the shallow waters near its coasts, but trawler fleets operate deep-sea fisheries as far afield as the Barents and west Greenland seas. The annual catch, mainly of cod, herrings, haddock, and mackerel, is about 800,000 tons. A number of seaports—notably Aberdeen, Hull, Grimsby, Lowestoft, and Fleetwood—engage vigorously in this activity. The chief fish market is at Billingsgate, London.

Industry

The United Kingdom depends heavily on industry to maintain the high living standards of its densely settled population. Industry consists mainly of manufacturing but also of mining and quarrying. This country enjoyed certain marked advantages for manufacturing industry: having built up an empire based on the sea routes and on naval supremacy and having amassed capital for investment, it became the home of the Industrial Revolution so-called which led to 'cheaper quantitative production'—the mass production, based on the use of machinery driven by steampower, of goods in factories. This revolution, which was accompanied by no less revolutionary changes in transport and agriculture, proved highly successful; indeed in the latter part of the nineteenth century Britain was truly the workshop of the world. It had then the advantage, as now, of considerable resources of Carboniferous coal which provided, and still provides, though less exclusively, a source of motive power and fuel (coke) for smelting iron. In this century competition from other great industrial nations has changed Britain's industrial status sharply: after 1913 it lost its predominant position, although it retains certain substantial assets—enterprise, skilled workers, a high educational level, coalfields still yielding nearly 180 million tons a year and being continually reorganized and mechanized and likely to stabilize production at about 160 million tons (*cf.* the peak year 1913, with 287 million tons), and a world network of commercial interest and goodwill. Thus the United Kingdom remains an outstanding industrial country, but faces the stern task of continually adjusting its manufactures so as to meet successfully world market conditions.

Coal-mining has continued as a major branch of the economy, but many uneconomic pits have been and are being closed, while mechanized mining intensifies in the more productive and often deeper seams. The best Scottish fields are now in Fife and the Lothians; the South Wales field has both relatively and absolutely declined; the West Midland field has little output today, while the bulk of coal comes from the Yorkshire–Nottingham–Derby coalfield, from the north-east coast, and from the East Midlands. The coalfields have ceased to draw industry and population to them as they did in the nineteenth century. They have ceased to yield a major item for export.

Similarly, the textile industry which took pride of place—*e.g.*, in 1880 and even in 1913—has contracted to become more highly specialized; important but of lesser scale than hitherto. So too the days are long past when Britain held first place in shipbuilding, although this industry is by no means insignificant.

The heavy metallurgical industry remains basically important to a wide range of steel-using industries: it no longer draws on ores from the Coal Measures, but imports high-grade ores to supplement its quarried supplies of low-grade ores derived from the Jurassic rocks of Lincolnshire, Northamptonshire, and Oxfordshire. But to the manufactures long produced and exported are now added many others which take the lead—motor vehicles, aircraft, and engineering and chemical products of many kinds. In addition, the United Kingdom depends on imports of crude petroleum, especially from Kuwait, but has used this need as a basis for a modern large-scale refinery and petro-chemical industry. The search for petroleum and gas beneath the North and Irish Seas continues, and substantial gas resources have been found beneath the North Sea, as also inland (as at Lockton, North Riding of Yorkshire): natural gas is already imported from the Sahara. And, since it must try to keep ahead in promising scientific and technological advances which have industrial applications, this country was the first to produce electricity from nuclear plants, as it has taken a lead in producing plants which derives fresh water from salt water. Needless to say, the United Kingdom has a wide range of light industries, many of which enter into world trade: textiles, leather, boots and shoes, hosiery, books, clothing, office equipment, and plastic goods may be noted among these.

Over the greater part of the country employment in manufacturing industry is below average: in other words, important industrial towns are not widespread but localized in specific areas where tradition and the law of comparative advantage are favourable. In the nineteenth century much industrial growth took place on the coalfields of the Midlands and north, additionally to that which continued in southern England. In recent decades, with less industrial dependence on local coal supplies and with road and rail facilities, many industries can be freer in their choice of location. Lowland England enjoys the preference, and in the Midlands and south-east the working population has increased thanks to the movement of labour from northern areas. The outstanding zone of manufacturing industries extends diagonally across England from Lancashire (with now diversified industries) and the West Riding of Yorkshire (with textiles, clothing, and metallurgical industries)

N

through the English Midlands (widely varied metal goods) to Gloucestershire (aircraft), Middlesex, and Essex. Within this belt Greater London, commanding so great a market and seaport, retains its share of some 20% of total manufactures. In Scotland Clydeside, with a hard core of shipbuilding and the many trades ancillary to this, is the outstanding industrial area; in Northern Ireland the County of Antrim, with shipbuilding of Belfast and linen manufacture in the Lagan valley, is the chief focus; in South Wales the coalfields have lost importance, but both heavy and light industries are located. The north-east coast, with its coalfield, steel, shipbuilding, engineering, and chemical industries, as well as the Potteries of north Staffordshire, are noteworthy areas of specialized industry.

Among efforts to modernize British industry, the better to increase its competitive character, are improvements in transport by the building of motorways, the nationalization of the railway system, and the construction of pipelines for petroleum and gas. In Scotland some small hydro-electricity plants are operating, two new road bridges—one across the Firth of Forth, the other across the Firth of Tay—are now open, and the introduction of new industrial projects —motor vehicles and pulp and paper—are efforts to foster industrial growth. This is part of a national policy which seeks to promote industries in those areas of the country where labour supplies are relatively ample and living standards are lower: this applies also to Northern Ireland, the north-east coast, and South Wales, where industrial development is increasingly located in the coastal areas. This last will soon become part of a Bristol Channel industrial area now that it is joined to England by the Severn road bridge completed in 1966.

The Place of the United Kingdom in Europe and the World

Throughout modern times the United Kingdom, despite or because of the British insular character, developed world-wide interests. These expressed themselves for a time in empire-building, but the British Empire has virtually disappeared, although British colonists have settled in many parts of the world (the United States, Canada, Australia and New Zealand, and elsewhere). Britain finds itself today the senior member in a world-wide Commonwealth, composed of independent peoples of variant ethnic, national, religious, and social type. Undoubtedly, since the United Kingdom needs industrial strength to support ever-growing trade across the seas, it seeks to join the Common Market, where the best prospects of trade expansion now lie. Although its trade with the Commonwealth is still sizeable, this now amounts to a decreasing percentage.

PROFESSOR W. GORDON EAST
Birkbeck College
University of London

CONCLUSION

Between the covers of this volume there have been brought together two aspects of the life of Europe. First the content was viewed as a whole and within its major regions, as described in the report of the four Conferences on the revision of Geography Textbooks[1]. Next—and this is the peculiar contribution of this volume—it was seen through the eyes of geographers in the different member countries of Europe, each describing his country as he would wish it depicted by authors and teachers in other lands.

Before closing the volume readers should perhaps also be reminded, if only in outline, that there is today yet a third perspective to the geography of Europe. As well as the continent and its individual countries, there are now certain organizations which embrace a number of individual countries and which appreciably affect their economic and political development. To round off this picture of Europe mention will be made of the more important of them[2].

For the geographer, perhaps the most obviously relevant of these organizations are the European Communities, comprising the ECSC (European Coal and Steel Community), the EEC (European Economic Community, or Common Market) and Euratom; and with these might be linked also in the near future EFTA (European Free Trade Association). The ECSC, for example, has established a common market for coal, iron, and steel, in its six member countries. The EEC aims at the formation of a general economic union between its countries through such things as the abolition of all tariffs and all restrictions on movement of workers, professional people, services, and capital, and through the adoption of common policies for agriculture, transport, and trade. EFTA, though within a looser framework, and with no implications of possible political merging, has a somewhat similar policy for seven countries outside the Common Market. These organizations inevitably exert a marked influence on the development of the countries of Europe—individually and as a whole.

---

[1] See *Geography Teaching and the Revision of Geography Textbooks and Atlases*, published by the Council for Cultural Co-operation of the Council of Europe—Series 'Education in Europe', II, 9—in 1967.

[2] For their distribution see Table, p. 191.

The three bodies which embrace a wider membership are of two kinds. First is NATO (North Atlantic Treaty Organization), which is primarily a defensive organization. It includes the United States and Canada as well as thirteen European states, and was formed "to safeguard the freedom, common heritage, and civilization of their peoples, founded on the principles of democracy, individual liberty, and the rule of law".

Neither of the other two bodies, the OECD (Organization for Economic Co-operation and Development) and the Council of Europe, is concerned with military defence. The OECD derives from the OEEC, an organization set up to administer Marshall Plan aid after the destruction of the Second World War. It aims at fostering economic co-operation among all its twenty-one members, and even of encouraging help to underdeveloped countries. The Council of Europe, which grew out of the Brussels Pact, and which gradually absorbed the cultural aspects of the later Western European Union, serves as a focus in all matters economic, cultural, and political for eighteen countries of Europe. It aims "to achieve a greater unity between its members for the purpose of safeguarding and realizing the ideals and principles which are their common heritage and facilitating their economic progress". It works through a Committee of Ministers and a Consultative Assembly of 147 representatives from national parliaments. It is, in fact, *the* European Forum. Its cultural activities, achieved through its Council for Cultural Co-operation (CCC), are witnessed, among many other things, by the organization of educational conferences such as those on the revision of geography textbooks and atlases, and by the sponsoring of publications such as this volume. One interesting feature of the CCC is that it does represent not only the member states of the Council of Europe, but also three other states which have signed the Cultural Convention—Finland, Spain, and the Holy See. Portugal took part in its geography conferences.

That Europe should be looked at from such differing points of view, particularly from that which stresses its unity as opposed to the viewpoints of its individual states, might suggest a measure of divergence. There are certainly some grounds for such fears. But, as suggested in the final paragraph of the Report already mentioned ". . . the accurate depicting of individual countries and the emphasis on the fundamental unity of Europe as a whole are essentially complementary. It is only by understanding the culture and the economic development of Europe as a whole that one can rightly appreciate the separate contribution of its individual states. Equally, the more geographers in one country understand fully and sympathetically the background and the aspirations and the up-to-date achievements of their neighbours, the more quickly is likely to grow that perception of a fundamental overall unity". The same theme was picked up by M. François in his introduction to this volume. "Each country is presented as seen through the eyes of one of its own geographers, but the work does not consist of a series of nationalistic panegyrics. . . . this book is intended, above all, to show that the old Europe . . . even seems to have recovered fresh youth and vitality."

It is true that some contributions may appear—not surprisingly—to lean slightly towards national pride. But in general it is hoped that, though not embracing all countries in Europe, they do underline both facets of the life of the continent, and that through them there emerges a picture of varied national individuality—even idiosyncrasy—yet set in a vigorous entity called Europe—a Europe still clearly distinguishable, through past history and present trends, from other continents of the globe.

MEMBERSHIP OF WESTERN ORGANIZATIONS

Countries	Organization for Economic Co-operation and Development (OECD)	North Atlantic Treaty Organization (NATO)	Council of Europe	Western European Union (WEU)	European Communities			European Free Trade Association (EFTA)
					European Coal and Steel Community (ECSC)	European Economic Community (Common Market)	European Atomic Energy Community (EURATOM)	
Belgium	*	*	*	*	*	*	*	
France	*	*	*	*	*	*	*	
Germany	*	*	*	*	*	*	*	
Italy	*	*	*	*	*	*	*	
Luxembourg	*	*	*	*	*	*	*	
Netherlands	*	*	*	*	*	*	*	
Austria	*		*					*
Canada	*	*						
Cyprus			*					
Denmark	*	*	*					*
Finland	†							A
Greece	*	*	*			A		
Iceland	*	*	*					
Irish Republic	*		*					
Japan	*							
Malta			*					
Norway	*	*	*					*
Portugal	*	*						*
Spain	*							
Sweden	*		*					*
Switzerland	*		*			A		*
Turkey	*	*	*					
United Kingdom	*	*	*	*				*
United States	*	*						
Yugoslavia	†							

This table was correct at June 1968

* Member.   A Associate.   † Finland and Yugoslavia have a special status in OECD.

Bibliography

AUSTRIA

Publications

SCHEIDL, L. (editor): *Wiener Geographische Schriften* (Verlag F. Hirt, Vienna; twice yearly).

SCHEIDL, L., and LECHLEITNER, H.: *Österreich—Land, Volk, Wirtschaft.*

Hirts Stichwortbücher (Verlag F. Hirt, Vienna, 1967; new editions biennially).

Mitteilungen (Österreichische Geographische Gesellschaft; three numbers yearly).

Statistisches Handbuch für die Republik Österreich (Österreichisches Statistisches Zentralamt, Vienna; annually).

Wirtschafts-statistisches Handbuch (Kammer für Arbeiter und Angestellte für Wien; annually).

Institutes

Institut für Österreichkunde, Hanuschgasse 3, 1010 Vienna.
Geographisches Institut der Hochschule für Welthandel, Franz Kleingasse 1, 1190 Vienna.

BELGIUM

Institutes

Institut Belge d'Information [IMBEL], 3 rue Montoyer, Brussels 4.
Government Institutes or Information Services: Institut National de Statistique, 44 rue de Louvain, Brussels 1.

FEDERAL REPUBLIC OF GERMANY

Publications

Geographische Rundschau (Georg Westermann Verlag, 33 Brunswick; monthly).

Der Fischer Weltalmanach (Fischer Bücherei, 6 Frankfurt; annually).

Statistisches Jahrbuch für die Bundesrepublik Deutschland, large edition (Statistisches Bundesamt, 62 Wiesbaden; annually).

Statistiches Jahrbuch der Deutschen Demokratischen Republik, large edition (Staatsverlag der Deutschen Demokratischen Republik, Berlin; annually).

Statistisches Taschenbuch der Deutschen Demokratischen Republik, pocket edition (Staatsverlag der Deutschen Demokratischen Republik, Berlin; annually).

Institutes

Internationales Schulbuchinstitut, 33 Brunswick, Rebenring 53.
Statistisches Bundesamt, 62 Wiesbaden.
Staatliche Zentralverwaltung für Statistik, Berlin (East).

FINLAND

Publications

Facts about Finland (Otava Publishing Company, Uudenmaankatu 10, Helsinki 10).

Atlas of Finland (Geographical Institute of the University of Helsinki and Otava Publishing Company, address as above).

Terra Fennica (Geographical Society of Finland, Hallituskatu 11–13 Helsinki 10).

General Map of Finland (Board of Land Surveying, Kirkkokatu 3, Helsinki 17).

Introduction to Finland (Publishing Company WSOY, Bulevardi 12, Helsinki 12).

Statistical Yearbook of Finland (Central Statistical Office of Finland, Annankatu 44, Helsinki 10).

Institutes, Societies, and Government Departments

Geographical Institutes of the universities in the following towns: Helsinki, Turku, and Oulu.

Geographical Society of Finland, Hallituskatu 11–13, Helsinki 10.

Geographical Society Nordenskiöld-samfundet, address as above.

Biological Society Vanamo, Mannerheimintie 16A, c/o E. Palmén, Helsinki 10.

Board of Land Surveying, Kirkkokatu 3, Helsinki 17.

Institute of Geodesical Research, Hämeentie 31, Helsinki 50.

Institute of Geological Research, Otaniemi.

Central Institute of Meteorological Research, Vuorikatu 24, Helsinki 10.

Hydrological Office, address as above.

Central Statistics Office of Finland, Annankatu 44, Helsinki 10.

Ministry of Education (International Affairs), Aleksanterinkatu 3D, Helsinki 17.

Ministry of Foreign Affairs, address as above.

FRANCE

Publications

Annuaire Statistique de la France (L'Institut National de la Statistique et des Etudes Economiques, 29 Quai Branly, Paris VIIe; annually).

Les Cahiers Français (La Documentation Française, 31 Quai Voltaire, Paris VIIe; monthly).

Images Economiques du Monde (Société d'Edition de l'Enseignement Superieur [SEDEG], 5 Place de la Sorbonne, Paris V^e; annually).

Institutes

Institut National de la Statistique et des Etudes Economiques (I.N.S.E.E.), 29 Quai Branly, Paris VIIe.

La Documentation Française, 31 Quai Voltaire, Paris VIIe.

GREECE

Publications

Geography/Atlas of Modern Greece, Vol. 1 (Atlas Publications, Athens). In Greek.

New Geography/Atlas of Greece, Vol. IV (Siropouli Brothers and C. Coumoundoureas, Athens, 1964). In Greek.

New Universal Encyclopedia, Volume *Greece* (Morphotiki Etairia, Athens, 1959). In Greek.

KOLIAS, GEORGE T.: *Historical Geography of Greece*. In Greek.

Economic Encyclopedia, Volume *Greece* (John Sideris, Athens, 1958). In Greek.

Bulletins of the Greek National Office of Statistics (O.N.S.G.). In Greek, English, and French.

Institutes, Government Services, Societies

Greek National Office of Statistics, 14 Lykourgou Street, Athens.

Institute for Geology and Subsurface Research, 6 Amerikis Street, Athens.

Greek Geographical Society, 105B Aiolou Street, Athens.

ITALY

Publications

Bollettino della Società Geografica Italiana (Rome).

Calendario Atlante De Agostini (Novara).

Bollettino mensile dell'Istituto Centrale di Statistica (Rome).

Vita Italiana. Documenti e Informazioni (Rome).

Institute

Presidenza del Consiglio dei Ministri, Servizi della Informazione e della Proprietà Letteraria, Via Boncompagni 15, Rome.

MALTA

Publication

Census of Malta (including Census of Agriculture).

Institutes

Department of Information, 24 Merchants' Street, Valletta.

Meteorological Office, RAF, Luga, B.F.P.O. 51.

NETHERLANDS

Publications

Statistisch Zakboekje (Central Bureau of Statistics, Oostduinlaan 2, The Hague; annually).

Holland, a Short Survey (Ministry of Foreign Affairs, The Hague). In French, German, Italian, Spanish, and thirty-two other languages.

Nederlando, nacio Okcidenta Europo (Ministry of Foreign Affairs, The Hague). Esperanto; also in Italian, Spanish, Polish, Serbo-Croat, and Afrikaans.

The Netherlands, Work and Prosperity (Ministry of Foreign Affairs, The Hague). Also in French, German, and Spanish.

Many thematic geographical publications in English, French, German, and Italian; information from: Information and Documentation Centre for the Geography of the Netherlands, Geographical Institute, State University of Utrecht (Dr H. S. Verduin-Muller).

Map of the Netherlands for use in schools (Ministry of Foreign Affairs, The Hague, in co-operation with the Information and Documentation Centre for the Geography of the Netherlands).

NORWAY

Periodicals

Statistical Yearbook of Norway (Statistisk sentralbyrå, Dronningens gate 17, Oslo 1).

Facts about Norway (Chr. Schibsteds forlag, Pilestredet 10, Oslo 1).

Norwegian Agriculture and its Organizations (Bøndenes forlag, Parkveien 37, Oslo 3).

Keyfacts—Norway's Industry (Norges industriforbund, Drammensveien 40, Oslo 2).

HELVIG and JOHANNESSEN: *Norway—Land, People, Industries—A Brief Geography* (Tanums forlag, Oslo 1).

Institutes or Government Departments

Contact for publishers and authors of educational books: Cultural Department, Ministry of Foreign Affairs, Oslo Dep., Norway.

Contact for teachers of geography in the secondary schools: Organisation of Secondary School Teachers, Section of Geography, Wergelandsveien 15, Oslo 1, Norway.

PORTUGAL

Periodicals from the Instituto Nacional de Estatística

Monthly Statistical Bulletin.

Statistical Yearbook, Vol. 1: Continent, Azores, and Madeira; Vol. 11: Overseas.

Agricultural and Food Statistics (annually).

Statistics of Foreign Trade (annually).

Demographic Statistics (annually).

Financial Statistics (annually).

Educational Statistics (biennially).

General Census of the Population (ten-yearly).

Relatório Anual, Vol. I and II (Banco de Portugal).

Geographica (Sociedade de Geografia de Lisboa).

Boletim Geral do Ultramar (L'Agència Geral do Ultramar).

Institutes

Instituto Nacional de Estatística, Lisbon 1.

Secretaria de Estado da Informação e Turismo, Palácio Foz, Lisbon 2.

Ministério das Finanças, Instituto Geográfico e Cadastral, Praça da Estrela, Lisbon 2.

Ministério da Economia, Secretaria de Estado da Agricultura, Serviço de Informação Agrícola, Av. António Augusto de Aguiar 104, 7° Lisbon 1.

Ministério do Ultramar, Agencia Geral do Ultramar, Praça do Comércio, Lisbon 2.

Ministério dos Negócios Estrangeiros, Comissão Nacional da F.A.O., Palácio das Necessidades, Lisbon 3.

Delegação Permanente de Portugal Junto das Nações Unidas, United Nations Building, New York, N.Y.

Delegação Permanente de Portugal Junto da Efta, 32 Chemin des Colombettes, 1211 Geneva.

Delegação Permanente de Portugal Junto da OCDE, 2 Rue André-Pascal, Paris, 16°.

Universidade de Lisboa, Centro de Estudos Geográficos, Faculdade de Letras, Cidade Universitária, Lisbon 4.

Associação Comercial de Lisboa, R. das Portas de S. Antão 89, Lisbon 2.

Associação Industrial Portuguesa, Praça das Indústrias (Junqueira), Lisbon 3.

Instituto Gulbenkian de Ciência, Fundação Calouste Gulbenkian, Rua D. João V, 30, Lisbon 2 (or Av. Berne, Lisbon 1).

Sociedade de Geografia de Lisboa, R. das Portas de S. Antão, 100, Lisbon 2.

Ministério de Economia, Secretaria de Estado da Indústria, Instituto Nacional de Investigação Industrial (Serviço de Documentação e Informação), R. Garcia da Orta, 68–1°, Lisbon 2.

SWEDEN

Publications

Statistisk Årsbok för Sverige (Statistiska Centralbyrån, Linnégatan 87, Fack, Stockholm 27).

Industria (Kungsholmstorg 1, Box 22105, Stockholm 22; annual international issue). In English, German, and French.

Svensk Geografisk Årsbok (Department of Geography, University of Lund, Sölvegatan 13, Lund).

Svenska Turistföreningens Årsskrift (Svenska Turistföreningen [Swedish Touring Club], Stureplan 2, Fack, Stockholm 7).

Information Centre

Svenska Institutet, Kungsgatan 42, Stockholm, Postbox 3306.

SWITZERLAND

Periodicals

Annuaire Statistique de la Suisse (Bureau Fédéral de Statistique, Berne).

Bréviaire Suisse (Kümmerly and Frey, Berne).

Statistiques et évaluations, concernant l'agriculture et l'alimentation (Secrétariat des paysans suisses, Brugg).

Bericht über Handel und Industrie (Schweizerischer Handels- und Industrie-Verein, Zürich).